THE LAST
OF
THE BUSHRANGERS

NED KELLY.

Frontispiece.

THE LAST
OF
THE BUSHRANGERS

*AN ACCOUNT OF THE CAPTURE OF
THE KELLY GANG*

BY

FRANCIS AUGUSTUS HARE, P.M.
LATE SUPERINTENDENT OF VICTORIAN POLICE

The Naval & Military Press Ltd

published in association with

Published by the
The Naval & Military Press
in association with the Royal Armouries

Unit 10 Ridgewood Industrial Park,
Uckfield, East Sussex, TN22 5QE
Tel: +44 (0) 1825 749494
Fax: +44 (0) 1825 765701

For a full listing of all N&MP titles, visit:
www.naval-military-press.com

MILITARY HISTORY AT YOUR FINGERTIPS

Online genealogy research:
www.military-genealogy.com

The Library & Archives Department at the Royal Armouries Museum, Leeds, specialises in the history and development of armour and weapons from earliest times to the present day. Material relating to the development of artillery and modern fortifications is held at the Royal Armouries Museum, Fort Nelson.

For further information contact:
Royal Armouries Museum, Library, Armouries Drive,
Leeds, West Yorkshire LS10 1LT
Royal Armouries, Library, Fort Nelson, Down End Road, Fareham PO17 6AN

Or visit the Museum s website at
www.armouries.org.uk

In reprinting in facsimile from the original, any imperfections are inevitably reproduced and the quality may fall short of modern type and cartographic standards.

CONTENTS.

CHAPTER I.
Introductory Remarks—Birth—Early Days at the Diggings—Unlicensed Diggers—Attacked by Fever—Keeping a Store 1

CHAPTER II.
Lieutenant in Victorian Police—Gold-Escort Duty—Catching a Burglar—All that was left of him—Brooks the Murderer—At the Buckland River Station—"Billy the Puntman"—In Charge of new Rushes—Border Difficulties on the Murray 19

CHAPTER III.
Power the Bushranger—His Escape—The Squatter's Gold Watch—£500 Blood-money—A Peacock as a Sentinel—Caught by the Heels—Some of Power's Adventures—His Sentence—Gamekeeper to Sir William Clarke ... 55

CHAPTER IV.
A Sporting Party on the Murray—"Winkle"—How to take Aim—After the Ducks—A Night with the Snakes—Kangarooing—A Runaway Bed 77

CHAPTER V.

The Kelly Gang—Ned and Dan Kelly—Steve Hart—Joe Byrne—The Origin of the Bushranging Outbreak—Search Party organized—Murder of Kennedy—M'Intyre's Escape —Arming the Police—Tracking the Gang—Close on them 92

CHAPTER VI.

Euroa Bank Robbery—Euroa—"Sticking up" Mr. Younghusband's Station—Mr. Macauley "bailed up"—The Hawker Gloster—Cheap Outfits—The Raid on the Bank— The Manager and Family made Prisoners—The Return to Mr. Younghusband's—The Retreat of the Gang and Liberation of the Prisoners—Explanatory Statement of the Author 112

CHAPTER VII.

The Police at Euroa—Aaron Sherritt—Jerilderie—Capture of the Police Station and Constables—Amateur Policemen— The Royal Hotel stuck up—Raid on the Bank of New South Wales—£2000 taken—Kelly's Autobiography—His Account of the Fitzpatrick Affair—Departure of the Gang —Return to their Haunts 137

CHAPTER VIII.

Aaron Sherritt—A Disappointment—At Mrs. Byrne's—A Twenty-five-day Watch—Manufacturing Brands—Sherritt's Revenge—A Letter from Joe Byrne—Whorouly Races—On Watch at Mrs. Sherritt's—Mrs. Byrne's Discovery—Breakup of the Camp—Arrest of Kelly Sympathizers—A Dynamite Scare—Aaron jilted 159

CHAPTER IX.

Mrs. Skillian's Hoax—A False Alarm—Searching the Warby Ranges—Among the Kelly Sympathizers—Ill and dispirited—The Tenant of the Haystack—Relieved after Eight Months' Camping Duty 203

CHAPTER X.

Black Trackers—Again in Charge with *carte blanche*—Aaron Sherritt's Doom—The Beginning of the End—Glenrowan—Sticking up the Hotel—Bracken's Escape—The Police on the Alert—A Dangerous Journey—Mr. Curnow's Adventure 227

CHAPTER XI.

The Attack on the Hotel—Wounded 267

CHAPTER XII.

From *The Age* Newspaper, 29th June, 1880—The Start—The Journey—A Timely Warning—The Gang surprised—Death of Byrne—Capture of Ned Kelly—His Statement—The Prisoners released—Renewal of the Fight ... 274

CHAPTER XIII.

From *The Age* (continued). Mrs. Skillian comes on the Scene—The Hotel fired—Rescue of Sherry—Fate of Dan Kelly and Hart—Statement of Various Prisoners made by the Gang—The Incident of the Cannon 291

CHAPTER XIV.

The Outlaws' Plans—Execution of Ned Kelly—Habits and Customs of the Gang—Katie Kelly's behaviour—Kelly's distrust of Hart—The Cost of the Destruction of the Gang 315

LIST OF ILLUSTRATIONS.

NED KELLY	*Frontispiece*
DAN KELLY	*To face page* 94
AARON SHERRITT	,, 140
JOE BYRNE	,, 192
STEVE HART	,, 240
NIGHT ATTACK ON THE GLENROWAN HOTEL	,, 270
NED KELLY IN HIS ARMOUR	,, 284
GROUP TAKEN DURING THE FIGHT	,, 308

THE
LAST OF THE BUSHRANGERS.

CHAPTER I.

Introductory Remarks—Birth—Early Days at the Diggings —Unlicensed Diggers—Attacked by Fever—Keeping a Store.

WHEN narrating to friendly audiences my experiences in the early days of the Colony of Victoria in what may be termed the "gold era," and some of the various incidents which occurred during my connection with the Victorian police, I have often been asked to give the records of them a more permanent form. After hesitating long, I have listened to those promptings, and, greatly daring, have ventured to address a wider range of hearers. I claim no more than to tell a plain, unvarnished tale, recalling from the reminiscences stored within my mind, events and incidents of by-gone days. Perhaps, had I written down the facts while the events were still fresh, I might have been able to put more spirit into my narrative, but my aim has been to keep within the record, to extenuate nothing, nor to set down aught in malice. I have endeavoured to refrain from mentioning names of private persons as much as possible, but, where I have found myself compelled to do so, I trust my references will raise no unkindly feelings.

Unfortunately, after the destruction of the Kelly gang, unpleasant feelings and jealousies sprang up between different officers engaged in the search, and interested persons kept adding fuel to the fire. In writing this account of the capture and destruction of the last of the Victorian Bushrangers, I have endeavoured to avoid locating the blame for the various unsuccessful attempts. We had a difficult task before us, and I feel sure each of us spared no effort to do his duty, though in thus acting all of us, no doubt, committed errors of judgment. In a matter of this kind every one has a right to his own opinion, and none but those who underwent the hardships we did can have any idea of our sufferings during the months we were in pursuit of the outlaws.

It seems hardly possible to imagine that ten years ago a field-gun was being dragged up Collins Street,

Melbourne, to blow down an hotel, which practically was little more than a wooden hut, within two hundred yards of one of the principal stations on the main line of railway between Melbourne and Sydney, as the last resource for the capture of four men, who for the previous two years had set law, order, the government, and police at absolute defiance.

Nor is it much more easy of credence that the capture of this gang should have cost the state, from first to last, over £115,000. And yet these are facts which cannot be controverted.

The first feeling that will arise in the minds of English people on reading this, will be one of wonder. How came it that four men should have been able for two years to carry on their career of crime unchecked? And what were the police doing? The police, and I speak from actual knowledge, were doing their "level best." A reward of £8,000 was offered for the capture of the men, dead or alive, and there was *kudos* and promotion to be gained. But there were peculiar difficulties connected with this undertaking; difficulties which could arise in no other country. Firstly, it must be remembered that these men were natives of, and were brought up in, the district in which they carried on their depredations; they knew every inch of the ground, bushes, and mountains; they had hiding-places and retreats known to few, if any, but themselves, and they were acquainted with every track and by-path. Secondly, the sparseness of the population outside the towns must be taken into consideration. These men might commit an act of violence in a town, and disappear into the bush, where they might, with the knowledge of the locality at their command, ride hundreds of miles without coming near a dwelling-house, or meeting a human being, and thus obliterate all traces of themselves for the time being; and lastly —what aided them more than anything else—they commanded an enormous amount of sympathy among the lower orders. It was a well-known fact that they had friends and adherents, either open or semi-veiled, all over the colony. The families of the Kellys, Hart, and Byrne were large ones, and members of them were to be found scattered over all the district ever ready to provide asylum, or furnish information as to the movements of the police. And outside their own families the sympathy they obtained was almost as great, though it was of a more meretricious order. The gang was lavish with its money. They subsidized largely, instituting a body of spies known by the name of "Bush telegraphs," who kept them fully informed of every movement of the authorities, and aided them on every possible occasion to elude capture.

And apart from this money consideration there was a further one, which appealed quite as effectively to their humble admirers. The gang never behaved badly to, or assaulted, a woman, but always treated them with consideration and respect, although frequently compelled by the exigencies of the situation to put them to considerable inconvenience. In like manner they seldom, if ever, made a victim of a poor man. And thus they weaved a certain halo of romance and rough chivalry around themselves, which was worth a good deal to them, much in the same way as did the British highwayman during the last century.

And now, with these few necessary words of explanation and introduction, let me get at once to my story, and the events which led to my being connected with the capture of the last of the Bushrangers.

I was born at the Cape of Good Hope, at a small village called Wynberg, about eight miles from Cape Town, and near the celebrated vineyards of Constantia. I was the youngest son of a family of seventeen! My father was a captain in the 21st Dragoons. The whole of his regiment was disbanded at the Cape; all the officers settled down amongst the Dutch inhabitants, and nearly all of us were born at Wynberg. When I left school I joined a brother who had a sheep farm, with which he combined horse-breeding and agriculture. After I had been on the station four or five years, I disliked the life so much that I was persuaded to emigrate to Australia. I arrived in Melbourne on 10th April, 1852, about six months after gold had been discovered. I did not know a soul out there then, and after a short time went on to Sydney, where I found a few people to whom I had letters of introduction.

After staying in Sydney a few months I returned to Melbourne with two mates whom I had picked up there, one a fellow-passenger I met going to Sydney. The voyage lasted seventeen days. My other mate was a runaway convict from Norfolk Island. He had been employed as workman and gardener in my other mate's family, and was a very hard-working old scoundrel. Melbourne at this time was a place to be remembered; the scenes that occurred in the streets and in the hotels would hardly be credited. The principal objects throughout the day to be seen in Collins and Bourke Streets were wedding-parties. Diggers used to come from the diggings with pounds' weight of gold, for the purpose, as they called it, of "knocking it down," and they managed to do this in a marvellously short space of time. You would hear of a man calling for two or three dozen of champagne (£1 per bottle), throwing it into a tub, and having a bath in it. Again, men would call for two slices of bread, put a ten-pound note between them, and eat the note and bread as a sandwich. Hardly a day passed without seeing six or seven wedding-parties driving up and down Collins Street, dressed in most gorgeous attire. It was said the same women were married to different men over and over again. When the man had spent all his money he would go back to the diggings to make another "pile," and when he had made it he would return to Melbourne. In those days there were no hotels, theatres, or places of amusement on the diggings, and any one who wanted any enjoyment had to run down to Melbourne. Gold was easily got—a man had only to sink a hole from four to twenty feet deep, and if he was on the "lead," the probabilities were he would get some pounds' weight of gold. At this time it was most difficult to secure any accommodation in Melbourne. You might offer any sum of money you thought fit, and yet not procure a corner to sleep in. I happened to get a bed at Hockin's Hotel, at the corner of Lonsdale and Elizabeth streets. I was awakened in the night hearing some one who was being garroted calling out for help; but help there was none. The colony was infested with convicts from the other colonies, and the most daring robberies in the streets of Melbourne were of nightly occurrence.

My two mates and I started with our swags on our backs from Melbourne to Bendigo, and camped out all the way up. The roads were very bad, and it was impossible to get a conveyance, so we humped our swags. As we went we joined in with large parties of men, all bound in the same direction as we were, for the purpose of our mutual safety. All along the road we heard of gangs of bushrangers sticking up parties of men. The dreaded spot on the road was the Black Forest, between Gisborne and Woodend. Having passed that we were tolerably safe. It took us eight days to reach Bendigo, and we pitched our tents on Golden Gully. Our first duty was to take out a licence to dig for gold, which cost us 30*s.* each, and then to sink a hole, which we bottomed, and took two or three ounces of gold. We then sank another, but were not so successful. About this time a new rush broke out at a place not far from Golden Gully, called Kangaroo Flat. We left our tent pitched in the same place, and went off to peg out a piece of ground, and set to work to sink a hole. This we bottomed, but it was also a "shicer." We sank another, and found it a little better, and got a few ounces out of it. All the diggers were very unsettled. It was the general belief that a mountain of gold would be discovered, and every one was anxious to be first in the rush, so as to mark out a portion of the mountain. Rumours of new finds frequently reached us, but those that were far off always appeared the most attractive somehow.

I must give some idea of the life on the diggings in those days. The parties consisted of from three to six men. One had to cook for the week, turn about. The leads of gold were always found in the gullies, and on each side of these gullies the diggers pitched their tents. Every party was provided with firearms, and at night it was the custom to fire off and reload them after dark. It was a peculiar sight to see the fires lighted all round each tent, and the diggers sitting about, and many of them having lighted candles as well. Bendigo in those days consisted of an irregular number of stores and tents erected where Sandhurst is now built. My ex-convict mate turned out to be an excellent workman, and would do anything for me. He always volunteered to undertake my part of the cooking, and was famous for his "damper," which was baked in the ashes. As there were no bakers in those days we had to bake our own bread. There was a quartz reef in Ironbark Gully, at the back of Bendigo. On Sundays we went there with a hammer and broke off a handkerchief full of specimens, which were quartz covered with gold. This reef belonged to no one, and any one might have taken possession of it. Quartz-crushing was unknown in those days, and I believe since then this same reef has yielded several hundred thousand pounds' worth of gold.

After staying at Bendigo for a month or so we heard of a new rush at the Ovens. So off we started to try our luck. The distance was great, but that only lent all the greater charm to our prospects. We had engaged a dray to carry up our swags, and were to have started off on a certain day, but owing to some reason we were delayed; so, being of an active disposition, I started off to a little gully by myself to prospect it. I took with me my pick, shovel, and tin dish; it was not 200 yards from my tent. In the evening I returned to my mates with ten ounces of gold. We held a consultation as to whether we should remain or go to the Ovens, and, I regret to say, we decided to leave Bendigo and the new claim I had discovered, and go to the Ovens. Accordingly off we started, early next morning. It took us ten days to get to Beechworth, but being a large party we had a jolly trip. We arrived at Read's Creek—a few miles below Spring Creek, as it was called in those days, but now known as Beechworth—a few days before Christmas, 1852.

The first thing, we set to work to make our Christmas dinner—I remember it as though it were yesterday. I bought the materials for a plum pudding; for a dozen of eggs I gave £1. I forget the prices of the raisins, &c., but I shall never forget the pudding! We boiled it for twenty-four hours!— it took us a week to digest—it was as hard as a cannon-ball!—it lasted a long time, and was something to remember! When we arrived at Read's Creek we found it in a most excited state. The diggers were up in arms against the Government officials, and whenever a policeman or any other Government servant was seen they raised a cry of "Joe-Joe." I never heard the origin of the word. The cause of this excitement was in consequence of a digger having been accidentally shot by a policeman, as he was obeying some order of a warden who was settling a dispute.

It appeared that the warden had directed an armed policeman to eject a man from a claim, and in stepping down he slipped, and his carbine accidentally went off, killing a digger who was standing on the bank of the claim. There was a general muster of the diggers immediately, and they hunted the warden and policeman off the ground, pelting them with stones, and for some weeks no official was to be seen on these diggings. My party happened to arrive at Read's Creek a few days after the accident had happened. The diggings at Spring Creek were quite different to Bendigo. The ground was very wet, and we sank what we called paddocks. The sinking was not more than twelve to fifteen feet deep, and the paddocks generally twelve feet by twelve feet. Not only did we find gold there, but large quantities of tin, in the shape of black sand, which was allowed to run down the creek. Eventually this black sand was collected, and as it was very valuable, large quantities were sent to Melbourne.

After working about a month at Read's Creek, a new rush was started at the head of Spring Creek, which was called "Madman's Gully." We started off there. By this time we had learned enough to know the best place to mark out a claim, and certainly found the richest hole we had yet had. The sinking was about fifteen or twenty feet, but gold was seen in a vein running through the wash-dirt. I used to pick out a match-box full of nuggets every day. I forget the exact quantity of gold we got out of it, but my own share came to more than £800 after the gold was sold.

We got very tired of paying thirty shillings a month for our licences, and only took out one licence between the three of us, trusting to chance to avoid the police when they were out digger-hunting. I remember on one occasion having great difficulty in doing so, and giving them a great chase after me. We had only the one licence, and suddenly found ourselves surrounded by a large body of police. I saw them observing us. I had the licence in my pocket. My mates had none. So off I started across the diggings to a hill on the side of the lead. My two mates stood where they were. The police, seeing me endeavouring to hide from them behind some rocks, tried to follow me; but their horses were unable to face the rocks. They all came after me, and in about ten minutes I was overtaken. The man who caught me demanded my licence, and I quietly produced it from my pocket. They asked me why I had run away. I answered, I was always afraid when I saw a policeman. In the meantime, my two mates, who had no licences, escaped, and we got off that month. The next month I was walking into Spring Creek with one of my mates, having left the other man with the licence behind. Suddenly the police were on us, before we could make an escape; they immediately demanded our licences. We made some excuse about not being able to pay for them, so we were handcuffed, and made to march back, whilst other non-licensed diggers were searched for. None were found, and when about four miles from the Spring Creek camp our captors asked us if we would promise to take out our licences if they let us go. We said yes. The handcuffs were taken off, and we were allowed to go free. I could give many instances of the iniquitous law of arresting diggers because they had not taken out a licence; but I have given two instances of my personal experience.

Our clothes were washed in a very simple manner. A flannel shirt lasted a week, and when washing-day arrived was tied to a root of a tree in the creek and left there for three or four days, then hung out to dry. We remained at these diggings for about three months. I was then attacked by a low fever and was gradually becoming weaker and weaker every day, until the doctor at last suggested I should leave the diggings and go to Sydney. I was terribly weak, not being able to walk more than a yard, so my mates found a dray bound for Wangaratta, and put me on top of the load that was going to town. The shaking of the dray was fearful. However, we arrived

ATTACKED BY FEVER.

that night at a place called Tarrawingee, about ten miles from Spring Creek. The weather was very warm, and we camped under a fine tree. The draymen on the roads in those days had great difficulty to prevent their horses being stolen, and the unfortunate men, after driving all day, had to watch half the night to protect their horses. At daybreak the drayman got up and made some tea. He offered me some, but I could neither eat nor drink, so he left me to get his horses, not returning till late in the afternoon.

Whilst under that tree a circumstance occurred I shall never forget. After the drayman left me a crow took up a position on a branch near me. And as the day wore on closer and closer he approached me, calling out unceasingly, "Caw, caw," as I thought to encourage other crows to come to a feast. As he became bolder I got in a terrible fright that my eyes would be eaten out before I died. So I exerted myself to drive him away, but he seemed to know I was too weak to do him any harm. At last I worked myself up to such a state that I forgot my illness and only thought of "going for" the crow, and I kept him off until the drayman returned. From that hour I improved. The next day we reached Wangaratta, where I remained a few days, until I was strong enough to bear a journey in the two-wheeled dog-cart, or mail cart, the only conveyance running in those days. I fastened a strap round my waist, sat with my back to the horses, and so went down to Sydney. My two mates soon afterwards dissolved partnership, and I never saw the escaped convict again.

After remaining in Sydney some three or four months, I met a cousin of mine, a Colonel Butterworth, who was the Governor of Singapore. He had come from Singapore, and advised me to get some settled employment, and as I knew no one in Melbourne, he promised to do his best for me. If I came with him to Melbourne, he thought he might be able to get me into the Government Service. I said I would prefer a cadetship in the Victorian police, as I was anxious to go in pursuit of bushrangers who were overrunning the colony.

I accompanied my cousin to Melbourne, but when he reached Queenscliff, he found a steamer going to Hobart Town, where he had left his wife, so he gave me letters to Mr. Mitchell and Mr. Latrobe. However, I got no satisfaction from either of them, so I went off to the Warranga diggings again, falling in with a Mr. G. D. M'Cormick, a native of Canada, and we agreed to be mates and work together. I must mention an extraordinary coincidence with regard to M'Cormick. He was born in Canada; I at the Cape of Good Hope. He was born on the 4th October, 1830; so was I. We parted from each other for many years, and in 1882 we were both appointed police magistrates for the colony of Victoria.

I met a man from the Cape there who had opened a store, a Mr. Barn (my father used to buy his snuff from his father at the Cape), and we used to sleep in the store for his protection. At that time I got an insight as to how grog was brought to the diggings (it was prohibited in those days). Flour was imported from America in barrels; and when it reached Melbourne a two-gallon keg of spirits was put in the centre of the flour, and the barrel with its double load was sent off to the diggings. The fine for having spirits in your possession was £50, and all the liquor confiscated. My Cape friend, wishing to pay a visit to Melbourne, asked me to take charge of the store during his absence. I did so, and served out tea and sugar to his customers, bought gold, and carried on the business for over a fortnight. My mate and I barely got enough gold to pay our expenses. I found the store-keeping a much pleasanter occupation.

About three months after I had been at Warranga I received a letter from my cousin, telling me he had seen Mr. Mitchell, the Chief Commissioner of Police, and he had given me a commission in the mounted police. I lost no time, and called on Mr. Mitchell (afterwards Sir William H. F. Mitchell), and he appointed me lieutenant in the Victorian police, 1st January, 1854.

CHAPTER II.

Lieutenant in Victorian Police—Gold-Escort Duty—Catching a Burglar—All that was left of him—Brooks the Murderer—At the Buckland River Station—"Billy the Puntman"—In Charge of new Rushes—Border Difficulties on the Murray.

I JOINED the police force on the 1st January, 1854, as a lieutenant. I was sent off at once to the Ovens district, and my first duty was to take charge of the gold escort from Beechworth to the Buckland. In those days there were few roads and no bridges, and the creeks had to be crossed the best way we could manage. The gold was carried down on packhorses and mules, each horse carrying from 1500 to 2000 ounces in saddle-bags. Frequently we had to swim the rivers. Some of the streams were very rapid, and when flooded were most dangerous to cross. On one occasion I lost two pack-horses; they were washed over a log below the crossing place of the Buckland River, and we never saw them again, although we searched for them for some days. Fortunately there was no gold on their backs. The gold used to be placed in saddle-bags, and sealed up, and we generally had four pack-horses or mules to carry it.

On one occasion, on our return journey, we found one of the creeks so flooded that it was quite impossible to cross without the danger of losing some of the men and gold. I took the men half a mile higher up the creek than the usual crossing place, and opening the saddle-bags containing the gold (the gold was always put in small chamois leather bags inside the saddle-bags), gave a few bags to each of the men to put inside their valises, telling them I expected each man to do his best to cross the stream, which was about fifty or eighty yards wide. I gave instructions that they should unbuckle their swords, and carry them under their arms, so that, in case they were washed down the stream, they could get rid of them. I had with me a Mr. Morphy, one of the Wardens of the gold-fields, whom I had picked up on the road, between two rivers. He put himself under my charge. I told him to follow me, but to keep at a respectable distance, so that if my horse came to grief he might avoid the difficulty. Neither of us could swim, so we were a pretty pair to cross a river fifty yards wide. I started into the water first, telling my sergeant to remain where he was till all the men had got safely over. I had not gone ten yards when my horse, which was a very small one, got his fore legs across a log, and was unable to get his hind ones over. It was no enviable position for me, on a horse playing a kind of see-saw in a roaring torrent.

Morphy followed close on my heels, and his horse whilst swimming put his fore leg on my shoulder, as nearly as possible pulling me into the water. I leant forward, and in getting clear of me, the horse's foot caught the hilt of my sword, which tipped up the scabbard. It fell into the river, and there lay for more than a month before I recovered it. The men got across safely. One of them struck a log in the same way I did, and, the horse falling over, he swam ashore. The pack-horses, having no weight on their backs, were washed down a considerable distance, but all landed safely on the other side. The gold being replaced in the saddle-bags, we started off for Beechworth.

Later on, one of the pack mules got away from the man who was leading him, and bolted off with 2000 oz. of gold on his back! We halted, and I sent two men off in pursuit, but after half an hour's chase, one of the men returned, and said it was impossible to follow the mule, which had got into an impassable place in the mountains. He wanted to know what he was to do. I told him if he could not catch the mule he must shoot it, and secure the gold. The trooper galloped back to the place he had left, the other man watching the mule, and in less than twenty minutes I heard a shot in the mountains, and shortly afterwards the two men returned with the pack-saddle and gold on one of their horses, they having shot the mule, and I was obliged again to divide the gold amongst the men. About four hours after the usual time of arriving we reached our destination, Beechworth, and I never was more glad to get rid of the responsibility of anything placed under my charge than I was of that gold!

In 1855 I was staying for the night at a station owned by Dr. Mackay, on the Ovens River. Mrs. Mackay was very ill, and the doctor, who was a tall, slight man, was by no means strong.

The doctor had sold a number of horses, and had received cash for them. He had this money, some £700, in his house, and in some way this fact had become known to, amongst others, a most notorious burglar named Meakin. There were other visitors staying in the house on this night, a Mrs. H. and a

Miss D., the latter a niece of Dr. Mackay. I had a bed made up on the sofa in the dining-room. The front rooms opened with French windows on to the verandah. My room was between Dr. Mackay's and that occupied by the two ladies before mentioned. The house was away from the road, and no other building within miles of it. At about two o'clock in the morning the two ladies came to the door of my room and awoke me, calling out there was a man outside in the verandah examining his revolver. They said they saw him put a large knife belonging to the doctor, which was lying in the verandah, into his pocket. At first I thought the ladies had been dreaming, and I told them to return to their rooms, and I would go outside and see who was there. I hastily put on some clothes, and opening the French windows went outside on to the verandah, but could not see or hear any one. I went back to my room, telling the ladies I could see no one, and I thought they must be dreaming, and I begged them to return to their room, promising to keep watch, and listen if I could hear any footsteps. The ladies impressed me with the fact that on no account was Dr. Mackay to be disturbed, because Mrs. Mackay was so ill that any fright might cause her death.

The ladies retired, and I lay down attired as I was. Five minutes afterwards I heard the dogs bark. I began to think that some one must be about. Then I heard one of the ladies calling out, "Who is that at the window?" I sprang out of bed, opened the window leading on to the verandah, and saw the figure of a man running across the garden. I called on him to stop, at the same time following him through the garden. He fell; I did so also. In another moment we were up again; he ran through some vines, the branches entangling him. I pursued him, and again fell. At last he made for a gap in the garden fence. Taking a short cut I overtook him and laid hold of him, and down we both fell on the top of a heap of rose cuttings and other rubbish, I coming on top of him. He had his revolver in his hand. I had no weapon of any sort. My first thought was to secure his revolver. I laid hold of the barrel, whilst he held the stock, trying to cock the pistol. It was a Colt's revolver, and I knew my only chance was to keep the barrels away from my body. I struck him with my fist; with all my might I hit him with my left hand, blow after blow, between the eyes. The struggle was for life, and notwithstanding it was on the top of a heap of rubbish, principally rose cuttings, men never fought harder.

Once I rolled over, and the ruffian was on top of me, but with almost superhuman exertion I got on top once more. He endeavoured to throttle me by putting his hand in the collar of my shirt. Fortunately, it gave way. In many other ways he tried to disable me, but always failed. The struggle appeared to me to last for half an hour, but, I suppose, could not have been more than six or eight minutes. I did not call out for help, thinking the burglar would have associates, and that they would come to his assistance. Mackay, having been told by the ladies that I had the burglar, called out to me. I answered. The man, hearing this, immediately gave up the struggle, and I took his revolver from him. Whilst he was on the ground I several times felt him trying to get something out of his coat pocket, but prevented his doing so. When Dr. Mackay arrived I put my hand in and found a long dissecting knife which he had taken from the verandah, also a couple of straps. We took him to the house. I was completely exhausted, and left the ruffian sitting in the kitchen, and asked Dr. Mackay to look after him while I got my coat, as I had nothing on but my pants. Hardly had I got outside the door when the prisoner made a bolt. Dr. Mackay called out to me, and I caught him getting over the paling fence which ran between the kitchen and the house. I pulled him down and dashed him to the ground, and seizing a huge stone —the only weapon I could find—threatened to smash his brains out if he moved. Dr. Mackay then got some saddle-straps. We fastened his legs and arms, and sent to Beechworth for a constable. On being informed of this, the man, who proved to be Meakin, a notorious criminal, remained quite still until morning, when he was sent to Beechworth. Meakin told me he had heard that Dr. Mackay had sold a number of horses a few days before, having been paid £600 in cash for them, and it was his intention to have robbed him and tied his feet and hands so that he could not move till the morning, nor give information to the police—by that time he would have retired to the mountains. He said :—" I brought these straps you have bound *me* up with to tie Dr. Mackay's legs." We found his boots in the garden, with a large stock of provisions to which he had helped himself out of the store. He told me his intention was to have robbed Dr. Mackay, and if he had resisted he would have shot him; and he might, with the provisions he had secured, have remained in the mountains for weeks before he need have appeared again.

The prisoner was taken to Beechworth, and committed for trial on a charge of burglary ; there being many other charges of a similar nature against him, he was remanded to Kilmore. On his way there he made several determined efforts to escape. I was at this time stationed at Wangaratta, the first stage from Beechworth to Kilmore, and he stayed the night there. In those days the watch-houses were of a very primitive character—a slab hut with earthen floor. Meakin had leg-irons riveted on his ankles, and it was only natural to suppose no man could escape with these on, but he was not to be daunted. He was locked up in a building like the one I have described, and a sentry placed at the door, with orders to watch the prisoner during the night. There was a lamp inside the cell, and several times during the night I visited the place, found the sentry vigilant, and observed the prisoner rolled up in his blanket against the wall. Next morning we discovered that all through the night he had been working—trying to effect his escape. Underneath where he was lying there was a large hole in the ground. He put all the earth into his blankets, and as his body was proceeding through the hole this filled up the space in the blankets. Unfortunately for him, the night was not long enough, or else he would have escaped. I was glad to get rid of him, and sent him on next day to Benalla.

In those days there was no train, and the journey, which now takes four hours, then took six or seven days. It took five or six days to get him to Kilmore, and each night he made some effort to escape.

At Kilmore the lock-up was considered especially safe, and it was thought quite impossible for him to make his escape. By night a sentry was placed over him, but not in the day-time. One fine afternoon the watchman went to the cell to give the prisoner some food, when, to his horror and surprise, he found the cell empty, the man having escaped through the roof, leg-irons and all, and to this day he has never been traced or heard of. He must have got some friendly blacksmith to knock off the irons, and got clear into another colony. After the capture of Meakin, Dr. Mackay presented me with a handsome gold watch, which I have worn to this day, with the following inscription upon it:—

Presented to Lieutenant Francis Hare for his gallant capture of an armed bushranger at Tarrawingee, the 23rd of June, 1855.

About the year 1857 a store was burnt to the ground not three miles from Dunolly. Some of the property had been dragged out and was in possession of the police, and the outhouses connected with the store had also been saved. The owner of the store was addicted to drink, and as he was missing it was generally believed that he had been burnt, as his body was nowhere to be found. The coroner of the district was communicated with; he came to the spot, and pointed out to the police some calcined bones amongst the *débris*. He ordered a box to be brought, and he and the constable set to work to collect the bones, and taking them to the nearest hotel, called a jury. and held an inquest. The coroner declared them to be the bones of a human being, and the inference was drawn that they were all that remained of the missing owner of the store. A verdict of accidental death was recorded, the friends of the deceased procured a coffin, and Jemmy being a favourite in the district, a great number of sorrowing and sympathetic persons followed the remains to the grave. A few days afterwards the police were ordered to sell all the effects of the deceased. A public auction was held, and the rescued property was disposed of.

At the auction it was rumoured that the deceased was known to have some underground place where he kept his money, and on the strength of this report a large sum was given for the ruins. A day or two after the sale the purchaser made the discovery of an underground passage beneath the store, and found the body of the deceased lying there! He had evidently, on perceiving the fire, gone down to secure his money hidden there, and got suffocated by the smoke, the whole burning mass having fallen in and prevented his escape. It was then found out that, in the store that was burnt, a number of hams had hung from a beam, and it was from underneath this beam the bones had been collected, upon which the coroner and jury had held the inquest, and which the sorrowing friends had followed to the grave. The purchasers of the ruins found a considerable sum of money in the underground passage. A second inquest was held on the real body, and the mourners again dropped the sympathetic tear. The coroner was at once called upon to resign. which he did!

About the year 1858 I was stationed at Maryborough. I had under my charge a large district, comprising a place called the "White Hills," which was about five miles distant from Maryborough. It was famous for the number of murders committed there. Hardly a week passed but two or three men were killed in the most cold-blooded manner. I recollect, one morning about four o'clock, being called up, and informed that a store-keeper named Lopez and my sergeant, named Barnett, had been shot during the night at White Hills. I immediately got up, and off I started to the spot. It did not take me long to ride the five miles.

The police station consisted of a portable building of one room fourteen feet square, a door in front, and two windows at the back. I found, lying on the floor in this building, the dead sergeant and store-keeper, and a wounded man named Brooks, suffering the most excruciating agony from a stab in the chest, about two inches in width. From a constable named M'Cormack, who was also stationed there, I got an account of the affair in the presence of Brooks. He said Lopez, the dead man, kept a store 100 yards from the camp. About one o'clock Brooks attempted to break into the store. He managed to get in, but was confronted by Lopez, who demanded who he was. Without replying, Brooks presented his pistol, and shot him through the heart. Lopez, after he was shot, sprang forward and thrust a large dagger, about two inches in width and twelve inches in length, into the man's body and left it there. Brooks ran away, and immediately a cry was raised, Brooks running across the diggings and passing within a few yards of the police station. Barnett, on hearing the cry, jumped up, and on seeing a man running away, he pursued and overtook him, when Brooks turned round, levelled his revolver at him, and shot him dead on the spot. A second constable (M'Cormack) followed Brooks, who again turned round and snapped his pistol in his face; fortunately it did not go off, and Constable M'Cormack knocked him down, took the pistol from him, and brought him to the police station, when he found he was mortally wounded. After M'Cormack had made this statement, I asked Brooks if it was true. He said, "Quite true." I asked him what had become of the dagger which Lopez had plunged into him. He said, "As I was crossing the diggings I drew it out and threw it away." I sent a man to the spot indicated by Brooks, and he brought back the dagger covered with blood. It had no bone or wooden handle to it. I asked Brooks whether it was in that state when he pulled it out of the wound. He said "Yes!" I made a search for the handle, but without success.

About day-break a great crowd of diggers came round the police station, and begged me to allow them to lynch Brooks before he died. I told them I could not possibly allow such a thing. They became most excited, and demanded that I should

DEATH OF BROOKS.

hand over the wounded man to them. I saw a long rope in the hand of a man, so I closed up the door of the building, with myself and the constable inside. The diggers then threatened to break in the door and windows, but I remained firm, telling them the unfortunate man could only live a few hours. The diggers then had a meeting, and decided to burn down and destroy all the tents where the thieves and murderers resorted on the diggings. During the time the diggers were trying to get hold of Brooks, he was calling out from the agony he was suffering, and they kept mocking him. His thirst was most intense, and he implored us to keep giving him water, which, of course, we did, and did everything we could to relieve his sufferings. About ten o'clock I was told that several tents and grog shanties had been set on fire. I looked out and saw men tearing up mattresses, and feathers being thrown into the fire, and all the furniture being broken up and burnt. About this time a large force of police had been sent to my assistance, and I was in some measure able to restore order. Brooks lingered on till about three o'clock in the afternoon, when he died in the most terrible agony. Lopez was an Italian, and lived in his store by himself, and was known to be a most determined man. The doctors held the *post mortem*, and said death must have been almost instantaneous, as the bullet had gone through his heart. The missing handle of the dagger was found by the medical man in Lopez' clenched hand. A tragic occurrence took place at the inquest. It was held by the coroner in a place used as a theatre, the jury sitting below the foot-lights. Three inquests had to be held, one on Lopez, the second on Barnett, and the third on Brooks. The inquest on the latter was not closed until nine o'clock at night, but while the coroner was taking the depositions the head of Brooks, which had been removed from the body, and put on the back of the stage, came rolling down, and fell on the ground among the jury. The coroner was anxious to keep the murderer's head, and the doctor, who held the *post mortem*, had placed the head at the back of the stage, forgetting that all stages slope towards the front. This skull was kept as a memento by the coroner until his death, when his widow sent it to me; and I now have it in my den.

I was sent in charge to the Buckland River station, about April, 1854, shortly after the new diggings were discovered there, and one of my first duties was to see that the diggers were all provided with licences. Having been a digger myself, I

A NARROW ESCAPE.

thought I would be able to circumvent the men who had no licences. The commissioner (as these officers were called in those days), named Mr. Hood, told me a few days after I arrived that he had been informed a number of men were working at the head of the river, and he proposed that we should take a party of police and explore the river some distance from the camp—at this time very little was known about the head of the river—so we arranged to take four mounted police, and go in search of diggers who were mining without licences. We followed them up to the junction of the two arms of the river. I took one side and the commissioner the other, each of us having two mounted constables with us. I was on the left side, and the commissioner with two men on the right. After going half a mile beyond the junction, I got on to a narrow track, the two men following close behind me. Suddenly I found the track getting more narrow and steep; my horse went faster and faster, until he could scarcely find ground to stand on, when away went his hind legs. I felt he was going over, and slipped my feet out of the stirrups, and as he reared or fell over, I saw a clump of grass on the edge of the precipice, and laid hold of and hung on to it. The horse rolled over and over a distance of 100 yards, until he fell into the river. He was terribly cut about, but with much difficulty we got him out, and led him home; the saddle was smashed to pieces. The commissioner on the other side of the river was amazed to see me walking down the hill. After hearing the clatter of horse, stirrup-irons, and stones, the two men, who were behind me, seeing the position I was getting into, pulled up their horses, and so avoided my misfortune. The commissioner suggested that we had better return to the camp, as we saw no diggers working on the river, so we went back, considering we had run a great risk to no purpose.

Another story occurs to my mind, whilst I was stationed at the Buckland. We had a most highly esteemed and worthy police magistrate, whose name I will not mention. His tent was fixed alongside of mine. It was the habit in those days for the police to be always on the alert for persons bringing liquor to the diggings, as no public-houses were then allowed except in townships. My men had made a large seizure, and the persons driving the drays were brought before the P. M., charged with carrying liquor for illegal sale. The whole seizure was confiscated, and in those days, instead of selling it, the magistrate directed that the liquor was to be destroyed. This order was made with regard to this seizure. On the following day I was about to carry out the order of the court, when the official came to me, and said, " Kaffir " (he used to call me " Kaffir " because I came from the Cape), " don't you think it would be advisable to keep the cask of port-wine that has been confiscated, for the poor frozen women about the diggings ? " The place at that time was snowed up half the winter. I replied, " I have no objection, but where shall we keep it ? " He replied, " Between our tents." I agreed to his proposal, and we fixed up the quarter-cask accordingly, and put a tap in it. From time to time the old women, and sometimes the young ones, came for a jug of port-wine, but one night I heard a trickle as if some one was drawing off a jug from the cask, and thinking that the sentry was having a pull at it (there was always a sentry over the gold-office, which was within a short distance of our tents), I got up as quietly as I could, opened the tent, and saw our worthy official drawing off a jug of port. I called out to him, " Are you drawing off a jug for some old woman at this hour of the night ? " He looked up surprised, and it was a sore subject for a long time. Some years afterwards I met him, and related to some friends in his presence the story of the port-wine, and, strange to say, he had quite forgotten all about it, and tried to make me believe he could not have been the official that I referred to.

The cold at the Buckland was intense on those days. The men were occupied half a dozen times during the night scraping the snow off the tents and off the police stables, which had merely a covering of calico, and there was great danger of the snow carrying away both tents and stables.

I was stationed at Wangaratta in the year 1855, before the bridge over the Ovens had been built. The only way of crossing the river then was by a punt, which was worked by a man named Billy. He used to be called "Billy the Puntman." This man was well known to be a confederate of the horse and cattle stealers in the district, but he always escaped detection. A bridge having been erected over the river, Billy's occupation was gone; and whilst I was travelling by coach to Melbourne in the latter part of the year, the mail-man, riding one horse and leading another with the mails, passed the coach some short distance from Greta, formerly called "Fifteen Mile Creek." The driver of the coach had hardly gone a quarter of a mile, when we found the mail-man standing on the side of the road without his horses. He told us that he had been suddenly stopped on the road by "Billy the Puntman," who

"BILLY THE PUNTMAN." 39

presented a double-barrelled gun at him, and he had ridden off as hard as he could go when he heard the coach approaching. In those days I never went anywhere without a revolver. I asked the driver of the coach if any of his horses were broken to saddle. He replied, "Yes, the near-side leader is a saddle-horse." I told him to take the horse out of harness at once, leaving the bridle on him. I made a pair of reins of a piece of rope, jumped on him barebacked, and rode in pursuit, as fast as I could go, in the direction Billy had gone. For some distance I easily followed the tracks of the two horses, but they led into stony ground, and not having much time to spare I lost the track altogether, and as I had to overtake the coach, being summoned to attend the Supreme Court, Melbourne, I galloped round the locality for some time, and then made my way into Benalla without seeing anything of Billy. I gave information to the police there, and got a fresh horse and saddle, and overtook the coach during the night near Euroa, reaching Melbourne in time for the Court. Billy was subsequently arrested at Albury, and a quantity of the stolen property, the proceeds of the robbery, was found on him. He was tried at Beechworth before Judge Forbes, and sentenced to ten years' imprisonment. He gave a good deal of trouble whilst being escorted to Melbourne, making several attempts to escape, but without success, and when he reached the last stage, Donnybrook, he tied a piece of blanket round his throat, and was found hung the next morning in the cell.

A good story used to be told in the early days of the Ballarat diggings, about a pair of boot-trees having saved the life of a police-officer. He was very ill with an abscess on his liver, and the doctors had all given him up. A police magistrate had shown him great attention both day and night during his illness, and when the dying man had abandoned all hope of recovery, he said to his friend, " My dear fellow, you have been very good to me during my illness, and I want to leave you something. I believe I am the only person in camp that has a pair of boot-trees, and when I die you may have them." The P. M. was very grateful. Next day he came quietly into the sick-room, thinking his friend was dying or dead. He picked up the boot-trees and was in the act of taking them away, when the supposed defunct, who had been watching him, made a sudden start up, and called out, " Come, come, Mr. P. M., you just leave those trees alone. I am not dead yet." The sudden start burst the abscess on his liver, and he recovered. Years afterwards the boot-trees used to be shown as the "life-preservers."

For four or five years I spent my time in taking charge of "new rushes." In these days many people do not even know what a "new rush" means, so I will try to describe one. Back Creek, now called "Talbot," is seven or eight miles from Maryborough. I was stationed there shortly after it opened. Diggers were prospecting for gold all over the country, and when they discovered a rich deposit, would at once apply to the Warden for an extended prospecting claim, the holders of which were allowed a considerable-sized piece of ground, much larger than the ordinary miner who followed after him.

Most wonderful accounts would immediately be spread all over the district that some very rich ground had been discovered, and at once people would flock to the spot and mark out a piece the size allowed by the regulation, each one driving in pegs in the direction they thought the lead would run. The fabulous accounts of the great finds would be published in every paper in the colony, and people would flock in from all parts. Stores would be erected, theatres built—besides numerous hotels—streets formed, and within three weeks or a month there would be about 50,000 inhabitants on a spot where, perhaps, a month previous there was not a living soul besides the prospectors. This is exactly what took place at Back Creek. A police camp was formed and several constables sent out, and I was sent in charge of them. When a rush took place, the miners from all parts of the colony would make for it. Back Creek was not wanting in notorious villains of all sorts! I had been in charge of the police at many large rushes, but never in my life had I seen so many rogues and villains together as were collected there! The police were at work day and night, and found it impossible to keep down the crime that was being committed. Murders were of the most frequent occurrence. People were found murdered in their stores, and were shot on the highway. I never went out without my revolver, and when I retired for the night kept it always beside my bed.

I will give an instance of the kind of crimes that were constantly taking place. I was in my office, about three o'clock, and a messenger arrived, saying there was a terrible fight going on a mile away, and that a man had been killed. I mounted my horse, and on my way met a Dr. C.; I asked him to accompany me, and left orders for two constables to follow. Arriving at the place I found a crowd collected, and saw a man apparently dead, and beside him a piece of his skull about the size of a man's hand, with brains in it. I ordered the body to be removed into a tent. Some one said, "We are waiting until he dies before we remove him." I asked the doctor to examine him, and he said that he was still alive. The culprit who had committed the offence was sitting on a log close by, perfectly indifferent about the matter. I asked some of the bystanders how the man had been murdered, and was informed that the prisoner and the wounded man had had a drunken quarrel; the prisoner getting the worst of it, knocked his opponent down, and with an American axe chopped the piece I have described off his skull. I ordered his arrest and sent him to the camp, where he was charged and locked up. I remained half an hour waiting for the man to die, but, finding he did not do so, I gave orders that he should be removed at once into the tent, leaving a constable, and giving him instructions to remain there till he died. The doctor would not do anything to the wound. He said it was useless, as the man could not live. Next morning I went to see why the constable had not returned, and, to my surprise, I found the patient still alive and conscious, and gradually he got better. The skin grew over the wound, and some months afterwards he gave evidence against the offender at the Castlemaine Assizes, who was convicted and sentenced.

Another case I can remember. One night I was called about one o'clock, a man informing me he had shot two men whilst they were in the act of robbing his store. His story was that he had closed his place of business before going to bed, having made everything safe; but he was awakened during the night, and through the canvas partition saw two men with a light helping themselves to his money behind the counter. He took his revolver and, without moving, fired at one of the men, who dropped, and then fired at the other, who walked a few steps and also fell. He at once came to report the matter. I accompanied the man to his store, and there found the two men lying as described by the store-keeper, with the money beside them. The coroner was informed of the matter, a jury was summoned, a verdict of justifiable homicide was returned, and so the matter ended.

Another incident took place at Back Creek, which is most forcibly impressed upon my mind. One night the lock-up was crowded with prisoners. The lock-up consisted of two small rooms with a boarded-up space between them; within this space was the body of a dead man who had been found murdered on the road, and the supposed murderer was in the adjoining cell. My quarters not being more than twenty yards off, I could hear the sentry pacing up and down guarding the prisoners. I awoke during the night, looked out of my door, which I always kept open, but could see no sign of the sentry. I walked down to the watch-house, attired as I was—still I could see nothing of him. Thinking perhaps he had sat down and fallen asleep in the small apartment where the dead man was lying, I walked in quietly and listened, but could see or hear nothing. The sentry, who had happened to be behind the lock-up, hearing a noise, suddenly came round the corner, and on seeing me, in a moment cocked his rifle and presented it at me. I called out, telling him who I was. He dropped his rifle, exclaiming, " Oh! sir, I thought you were the ghost of the dead man, and I was going to shoot him!" From that time I was more careful how I visited the sentry.

It was my duty to attend the court daily and conduct the prosecutions of all persons charged with offences. I was in regular attendance, generally from ten o'clock till five or six in the evening. A great part of the night I spent instructing the men in difficult cases, and giving general directions as to how they should be managed. In those days we were not bound down by red-tape regulations, and there were no newspaper reporters inquiring into every act. We had a very limited number of men, and they were worked to death, but there were no complaints even when working for sixteen hours a day! The life was exciting; gold was obtained by the ounce, and there were hundreds of thieves preying on the hard-working miner. Theatres, concerts, dancing saloons, were open till twelve o'clock at night, and the scenes I have witnessed in them are beyond belief. During my whole career in the police force, I have never had a hand laid on me. Whether my height and size protected me, I know not. I have been present when fights and every imaginable disturbance have been going on, but no one has ever touched me. I have been stopped at the door of dancing saloons, and implored by my men not to enter—bottles were being thrown right and left—still not a soul has interfered with me, and I have managed to quell the disturbance. It was a common occurrence my being called up at night, and frightful outrages reported to me. My first question was, "Have you arrested the offender?" When the reply was "Yes," I would then turn round in my bed and fall asleep; the next morning I probably would have forgotten the circumstance until reminded by some one. The camp life was very pleasant on the diggings, each man had a separate tent to sleep in, and a large one was used as a mess-room, where all the officers in the Government service used to mess together, and spend most sociable evenings, but this state of things only existed at the head-quarters of the district, where there were a number of officers stationed.

Writing of mess-rooms recalls to my memory an occurrence which took place at Maryborough where there was an old waiter named Tom, who was very fond of liquor, and generally, before dinner was over, was so drunk he could not bring the coffee in. One of the officers undertook to find out where he got his liquor from, and he soon ascertained that when any officer called for a bottle of wine, Tom used to decant it and leave a third of the wine in the bottom of the bottle, so he devised a cure for this state of things. One night, just as Tom had decanted the wine, I ordered him to go quickly and get something from the kitchen, and whilst he was away, I jumped up and put a good strong emetic in the bottle, having previously mixed the emetic in some wine; I gave the bottle a shake and put it down. The next minute Tom returned to the mess-tent, took up the bottle, and marched off with it. He was watched when he left the tent, and was seen with the neck of the bottle to his mouth, drinking the contents; not long after we heard Tom roaring at the top of his voice, very ill.

Of course we had quarrels amongst the officers, and some ludicrous scenes took place. One night I had been dining out, and returned about ten o'clock. On seeing a light, I went into the Warden's tent. The Warden was not in, but the gold-receiver was sitting on the bed. I said—

"What is the matter? You are as white as a sheet."

He replied, "I have sent to the police magistrate to ask him to fight a duel with me in the morning."

I said, "Why, what has he been doing to you?"

"He has insulted me," he said, "in the most gross manner."

"Well," I said, "you need not look so frightened over it." The owner of the tent soon afterwards entered, looking very serious, and said, "I conveyed your message to H., and he says he will see you d—d first before he fights you!" He jumped from the bed, and became most courageous, and said, "I knew he was a coward, and I would have given anything to have had a shot at him." Nothing more came of the matter!

On another occasion a row took place over some cards, and a duel was to be fought early next morning between a police officer and a warder, the P. M. acting as second to the police officer. It was arranged that the duel should take place at daylight, next morning, but before going to bed the police officer called the sergeant-major to bring him twelve rounds of ball cartridge. He did so, and the pistol and cartridges were left on his table. Next morning the P. M., who was a very diminutive little fellow, went to the tent of the police officer, and awoke him from his sleep, and told him it was time to get up to fight the duel. The police officer had forgotten all about the arrangement made on the previous night, and jumping out of bed, caught the P. M. by the back of the neck, and pitched him out of the tent; the P. M. went to the Warden and told him he declined to act as second to the police officer, and so that matter ended. Notwithstanding all these larks, we had no end of work to get through, and we all took a great interest in our different duties.

Another anecdote recurs to my memory at Maryborough. There was a very large rush to a place called Chinaman's Flat, where a fearful amount of crime went on. Only two constables were stationed there, and they were kept at work both night and day. One night I was walking about seeing how everything was going on, when I met two detectives. They told me that they knew a notorious convict who had escaped from Tasmania, and that he was in a tent on the diggings, living amongst the worst characters. We decided to arrest him directly the moon went down, which would be about two o'clock in the morning. I arranged that one of the detectives and myself were to go to the front of the tent whilst the other detective kept at the back, in case of an attempt being made to escape. Directly we approached the front of the tent a shot was fired. We lit a candle, threw ourselves on the convict, and dragged him from his tent. There were two other men with him, but the detectives knew the man they wanted. No sooner had we taken the prisoner away than we heard of a rescue being arranged, and in a few minutes a crowd followed us. I felt sure we had a bloodthirsty set of villains to deal with, and I blew out the light in our lantern. We doubled back and sat behind a high bank of earth, at the same time putting a revolver to the convict's ear, and telling him if he gave the alarm we would blow his brains out. The mob followed in the direction they had last seen the light, and passed within a few yards of us. We then went in the opposite direction with our prisoner and took him safely into the camp. The police magistrate remanded him next day back to Tasmania, at the same time telling us we had carried out the most risky undertaking he had ever heard of. In the course of three years I had the management of five new rushes. It was the most exciting time of my life, and I was not willing to leave it, but was persuaded to do so.

When the Echuca railway was being built the New South Wales Government claimed the River Murray, and issued a proclamation that after a certain day all boats and dutiable articles found on the river would be seized and confiscated unless duly registered. One morning I was prosecuting in the police court in Melbourne, and the acting Chief Commissioner, Captain Mair, sent for me. I went to his office, and he told me Sir James M'Culloch wished me to start at once for Echuca with twenty armed policemen, and go as far as Sandhurst that afternoon. The instructions I received were but scanty, beyond that I was to protect all boats on the Victorian side of the river and dutiable articles that might be landed on the Victorian shore. I had a proclamation, signed by Sir James M'Culloch, to the effect that I would be responsible for all boats on the Victorian bank, provided they were given over into my charge. I started for Sandhurst, by the three o'clock train, and a ballast engine was provided for me, to convey me from Sandhurst to Echuca, where I arrived at four o'clock in the morning. At Echuca the town was in a great state of excitement, fearing their boats would be seized. I had the proclamation printed at once, and posted on the trees, and at nine o'clock in the morning got introduced to the New South Wales Customs officer, who was dressed up in gold lace and buttons from head to foot.

I had a conversation with him, and he told me his orders were to seize all boats that were found on the Murray. I told him my orders were to protect these boats against seizure.

I said, "Then I think we had better bring this matter to an issue this afternoon. I will start a boat down the river from opposite Moama to Echuca, on the Victorian side, with a load of dutiable articles; you come and seize them if you can." I asked him what he would do if he were prevented seizing the goods. He replied, "I would have to shoot any one who interfered with me." I said, "All right; I will get a buggy; you accompany me up the river, previously arranging to have a boat there, and I will send up some tea and tobacco, put them in the boat, and start them down the river."

I ordered my sergeant to take up a box of tea and a case of tobacco, and at three o'clock Mr. G., the Customs officer of New South Wales, and I drove up the river. I told him, whatever happened, we need not quarrel. He concurred, and away we started. When we got opposite Moama I found a boat ready for me. I ordered the sergeant to put the goods in the boat, and jumped in myself. Mr. G. walked down with a broad-arrow branding-iron, and said—"I seize this boat in the name of the Queen." I said, "I would strongly advise your not putting your foot in this boat. If you do I will throw you overboard." He said, "Do you mean it?" I replied, "I do." I then landed, telling the sergeant to take the boat down to Echuca and to keep away from the New South Wales shore. He did so, and was in no way molested, and landed the goods at Echuca. I then said to Mr. G., "I suppose now you intend telegraphing for orders to your Government." He said, "Yes, I do." I replied, " Let us do everything fair and above board; you show me the message you intend sending, and I will do the same." He agreed to this, and we each showed our respective telegrams, and in half an hour

I received a reply from Sir James M'Culloch to the following effect :—" So far all right; if Customs officer interferes further put him in the lock-up." Needless to say I did not show this to my quondam friend! Mr. G. did not receive any reply to his message. I remained at Echuca for a month, but nothing further transpired. I had a sentry day and night on the boats placed under my charge, but there was no further interference from the New South Wales Government, nor do I even know what arrangement was afterwards made between the two Governments. On my return to Melbourne Sir James M'Culloch, the Chief Secretary, sent for me and paid me the highest compliment on the manner in which I had conducted the business.

CHAPTER III.

Power the Bushranger—His Escape—The Squatter's Gold Watch—£500 Blood-money—A Peacock as a Sentinel—Caught by the Heels—Some of Power's Adventures—His Sentence—Gamekeeper to Sir William Clarke.

POWER was a desperate ruffian. He had been convicted several times of different offences. He was under sentence when he escaped from Pentridge, previous to his turning bushranger. He managed his escape in a most extraordinary manner. The prisoners were carting rubbish in a small go-cart from the stockade outside the walls. Power was one of the men drawing the cart. There was a large heap where they were tipping up the cart. Power got under the rubbish unobserved by the sentries. The other prisoners, taking no notice of him, drew the cart back, while Power remained in his hiding-place until evening. When the prisoners were mustered he was missing. Search was immediately made for him, and the spot where he had secreted himself was discovered, but he had disappeared. Information was given to the police, and every effort was made to find him, but without success. Power at once commenced his bushranging career. He told me afterwards his first idea was to get a change of clothing, as he had nothing but his prison dress. This difficulty was overcome by stealing a suit of clothes from a farm-house. His next trouble was to procure arms. He found a blade of an old sheep-shears, fastened it on the end of a long stick, and made a kind of a lance. With this weapon he started bushranging. Before long he came across an old gentleman riding along the roads, and he took a revolver and some money from him. Thus armed he began his career, which lasted over eighteen months. He was the most fortunate bushranger (so he considered himself) we ever had in Victoria, and he boasted of having stuck up thirty men in one day.

The plan he adopted was as follows :—He chose a suitable position along a main road, where he could be quite unobserved by passers-by. He would probably take a coach road, wait until the coach came within ten or fifteen yards of him, then call out to the driver to surrender—" Bail up, or I will blow your brains out," at the same moment pointing a double-barrelled gun at him. The driver in every instance obeyed his orders. The bushranger would then order all the passengers to throw up their hands, and one by one to get out of the coach, and stand on the road, and turn their pockets inside out, letting the contents fall on the ground; Power himself keeping them all at a distance of twenty yards. He then made them march into the bush and sit down on a log about thirty or forty yards distant from the road. He was careful to select a suitable position in which to place his victims, commanding a view of the road as well as of those he had already captured.

On one occasion he stopped the coach with six male passengers, and two females, and he remained on the road three or four hours sticking up every man who passed by, till he had thirty under his control; he then mounted his horse, which was hidden in the bush, and told his victims they might go home, he taking all the cash and jewellery they had in their possession.

Power used to take most wonderfully long rides, frequently covering sixty and seventy miles a day. He had hiding-places in the mountains where he kept spare horses, and if hard pressed would make for one of these. He informed me the secret of his success was that he had no companions and never spoke to a woman. When captured, he was full of anecdotes. He was a very vain man, and had in his possession extracts from papers referring to his exploits, and had not the least hesitation in telling of his different robberies, and how he had escaped the police. He was a thorough bushman, and knew every gap and hiding-place in the mountains. The police were out after him day and night for eighteen months, and no money nor trouble was spared to effect his capture, many of the best bushmen amongst the police being selected from all parts of the colony, and sent into the district he frequented to try and capture him.

Captain Standish sent for me one day, and told me that Sir James M'Culloch (the Chief Secretary) had directed him to instruct me to proceed at once to the North-east district, and gave me *carte blanche* to do anything I chose, and incur any expense I thought advisable. I at once wired to my clerk, who had a thorough knowledge of the district, and whom I had previously sent up to make some inquiries, to meet me at a certain spot in the bush on the following Sunday. I, accompanied by one of my brother officers, left Melbourne on Friday at six a.m., and reached the meeting-place arranged on Sunday evening. We had also secured the services of a black tracker, and we all remained that night at a squatter's station, some miles from Benalla, who had himself been stuck up by Power whilst engaged with his sheep on the run. Power had stolen the squatter's gold watch, which was an heirloom, and very much valued by the gentleman. He knew Power very well, and had been very kind to him, and as he naturally felt very much hurt at being robbed in this way, we could not have stayed at a house where we were more welcome. Power had sent a message to this gentleman (the squatter) that if he was anxious to get his watch he would return it to him if he sent £15. The difficulty we had to contend with was to get some trusty person, who had Power's confidence, to take the money to him and bring back the watch. After a day or two we were introduced to a man whom I must call L——. It was a very delicate matter we had on hand, but my brother officer, who was used to dealing with men of this kind, undertook the task.

The Government had offered a reward of £500 for the capture of Power, and my brother officer offered this tempting bait to L——. The man threw all kinds of difficulties in the way, but we both stuck to him, till at last he gave way and consented to undertake the task. We had no end of obstacles to overcome, but we were determined to succeed. The first thing we had to do was to find a route in the mountains where we could travel unseen, as Power had so many spies—"bush telegraphs," as they were called—throughout the district, that had we been seen by any one, our chances of success would have been small. The next thing was, to get the £15 from the squatter to send to Power. I put my initials on the coins, and we started away on Thursday morning, the party consisting of L—— as guide, my brother officer, myself, my clerk, and a black-fellow.

We left the station early in the morning, unobserved by any of the station hands, with one day's rations, as we expected to be in the vicinity of Power's whereabouts some time next day. We found our guide was a very bad bushman and was constantly losing himself, but my clerk had a good idea of the country, and we got on tolerably well. We travelled in a most inaccessible country, on the tops of mountains very thickly timbered, and with great difficulty managed to get through creeks, gullies, and sidlings. The first night we came upon a deserted house, which was locked up, but we put the black-fellow down the chimney and made him open the door. The only food we found was some tea and sugar, so we camped there that night, my brother officer and myself lying on an old bedstead with a sheep skin as covering, the clerk and black-fellow before the fire on the floor.

Next morning we caught our horses, which were hobbled, and while the black-fellow was catching them I saw a fowl on the roof of the hut, and with some difficulty I managed to secure it. Not wishing the black-fellow to see I had taken the fowl, I wrung its neck, tied it up in a bag, and fastened it in the front of the saddle used by the black guide. We had not been mounted ten minutes when I turned round and saw the darkie laughing very heartily. I said, "Donald, what makes you laugh?" He replied, "I 'mell him, I 'mell him!" I said, "What you 'mell?" He said, "Chicken, ha ha!" I asked, "Where?" "In my swag," he replied. I was very much astonished at his smartness. This was the only food we had besides a bone of a shoulder of mutton.

As I said before, we expected to have been near Power on the Friday morning. We rode all day, and about sunset arrived at a deep gully, where the party were to remain whilst L—— went to a farm-house to endeavour to ascertain whether it was safe to approach Power. The farm-house was occupied by a notorious family, two or three brothers, all of whom were convicted thieves and bushrangers. L——, on leaving, led us to believe that he would return early the next morning, as he had only to ride about ten miles. We made a meal off the fowl, but it was the poorest creature four men ever dined off. We had great difficulty with our horses, they were tired, cold, and hungry, as they had travelled two days with very little food, so we merely sat on a log all night waiting for daylight to appear, holding the horses. No tents or covering of any kind, except one rug amongst us!

Saturday morning came, and there we remained all day, without food. It was raining in torrents, and the cold was intense, and no fire. We sat waiting all Saturday, the water pouring down the sides of the mountain like rivers, but L—— did not return, and we began to think we had been made fools of, when about four o'clock in the afternoon we heard the sound of horse's hoofs, and to our great joy found it was L——. Our first greeting was, "What luck have you had?" He made no reply, dismounted, took a handkerchief out of his pocket, untied it, and there displayed the squatter's watch and chain. We saw at once that L—— must have had an interview with Power, and we made him relate all that had happened during the time. He told us the Quinns doubted his honesty in wishing to see Power, and he was obliged to remain there for a day before he could even broach the subject of an interview with him, but after a good deal of caution Quinn consented to one of his associates taking L—— to Power's hiding-place in the mountains.

These Quinns were the only people in the colony who knew where Power was hidden. L—— used to be a great companion of Power, and used to be paid well, both in horses and money, for any information concerning the movements of the police, but the temptation of getting the reward of £500 was too much for him, so he consented to sell his friend for the blood-money. We then took counsel with L—— as to the best course to adopt in order to reach Power's place of concealment. L—— suggested waiting till Sunday night, forgetting that our party had had scarcely any food for two days. He threw every obstacle in the way of our starting that evening, telling us that if we were seen about the Quinns' house that night he would be shot, and that it was quite impossible to pass the house, which we should have been obliged to do to get into the mountains where Power was, as the rivers were all flooded, and the house watched by dogs, so that neither man nor beast could pass without being observed, and if we were on foot we should certainly be torn to pieces. Besides this, he said there was a peacock which always roosted on top of the Quinns' house, and no stranger could approach without the bird giving notice by uttering a shrill cry.

However, we were all determined to start that night, and we did so. We arranged our plans so as to pass Quinn's house about two o'clock in the morning, thinking as it was Saturday night that they might have been up late, and would be asleep by that time. Just as we were starting a terrific storm of rain came on, and our horses refused to face it. L——, being superstitious, took it for a bad omen, but we made a fresh start after the rain had stopped. We had a difficult gap in the mountains to cross, and L—— was in a terribly frightened state, and would have given anything to have retracted his agreement, and bolted from us, but we were firm and severe, and threatened to shoot him if he attempted to escape. We got through the pass much quicker than we anticipated, thanks to my clerk, and found ourselves within five miles of Quinn's house at about nine o'clock at night. Here we resolved to remain till twelve o'clock, and then make a fresh start. My brother officer and myself spent most of the time in walking up and down endeavouring to get warm, leaving my clerk, Donald, and L——, with the horses.

We were greatly excited at the prospect of securing Power, as he had baffled so many officers and men for the last eighteen months. At twelve o'clock we mounted our horses, and L—— was to lead the way to the place arranged, within sight of the Quinns' house. When there, we could decide on what was best to be done after seeing the surroundings of the house. We started away and got entangled amongst high ferns, logs, and creeks. We kept on riding for miles, and at last found—whether designedly or othewise—that L—— had lost himself utterly. We were in despair! I asked the blackfellow whether he could find his way back to the point from which we started. He replied, "Yes, you have been going round and round all night." He then took the lead, and in half an hour showed us the log we had started from. We again set out, my clerk leading the way, as he alone besides L—— knew anything about the country, and in an hour's time we arrived in sight of the long-looked-for house.

We decided to leave our horses in charge of Donald, about 300 yards from the Quinns' house, while the four of us endeavoured to pass the house unobserved.

No sooner had we dismounted than a terrific fall of rain commenced again, which was very much in our favour, as the dogs no doubt would seek shelter, and the peacock put his head beneath his wing. It was a most exciting moment. Strange to say, we passed the door in safety, having to keep within a few feet of the house, where some of the biggest ruffians in the colony were sheltered. Very much relieved at having succeeded, we began the ascent of the mountain behind the house. L—— had given us a good description of the locality where Power was camped. He told us it was a most difficult place to find. He had followed a track for some time, and had dropped pieces of bark and leaves of trees, so that we might know it again. He also described a hollow tree along the track, with a few old rags in it, within 200 or 300 yards of the spot where Power had his gunyah. We searched and searched for this track, but could find no trace of it. Our excitement was growing intense. It was just getting daylight, and it was more necessary that we should reach Power if possible before he awoke, as, in addition to being well armed, the country was so rugged that if he saw or heard us approach he could escape, and it would be next to impossible to find him.

In despair we held a council of war, and I suggested that the black-fellow should be sent for to endeavour to find the tracks of L—— and his friend on the previous day. My clerk opposed the idea of leaving our horses without protection, as they were sure to be stolen or let loose. But both my brother officer and I agreed that the black-fellow should be given a trial; so we sent the clerk back alone to get the black-fellow, and strange to say, they managed to pass unmolested or observed by the house, without either rousing the dogs' or peacock's attention. All this time my brother officer and self had our work to do, endeavouring to look after and quiet L——, who did nothing but cry, and try to escape from us. I never saw a man in such a terrible fright!

We thought the black man could be of little use after such a heavy rain. However, he appeared to get on a track of some sort, and followed it till he came upon the hollow tree described by L——, with a bed inside it. My brother officer, who was with the black tracker, beckoned me and pointed out the tree. I then said to Donald, "Can you see any smoke?" for we imagined Power by this time would have been up and had his fire alight. Donald replied, "Yes, fire up there along mountain." We started off at once in the direction the black-fellow pointed, and came upon a track, leaving L—— at the hollow tree. We ran up a steep hill and saw the smoke ourselves. We continued running, my brother officer leading the way, till we saw the fire and a kind of shelter under some gum trees, and as we approached I saw a pair of legs sticking out beyond the shelter. I went straight up to the legs, revolver in hand, and, in less time than I can write this, seized hold of the ankles, and pulled the man from under the shelter and away out of reach of his firearms. He was fast asleep, and uttered a tremendous howl, like a man in a nightmare, but there he was lying helpless at our feet. The first words he said were, "What police are you, and how did you get up here?" I replied, "We came from Melbourne, and passed the Quinns' house;" he said, "No fear, you could not have passed without the dogs and peacock giving the alarm." I replied, "We did pass there." The clerk put a pair of handcuffs on Power, then went to look after the horse. Power, meanwhile, dressed himself, and told us he had a presentiment that night, somehow, that something would happen to him, and hardly closed his eyes all night. At daylight, he got up and lighted his fire, and put on a "billy" of water to boil, and while waiting had lain down and fallen asleep.

We then searched his tent, and found his six-chambered Colt's revolver, loaded; and from the ridge-pole of his tent hung his double-barrelled shot gun, fastened by two strings, commanding a view of the path we had come up. It was loaded with slugs, and doubtless had he been awake, we should have had the contents in our bodies; but it was not to be.

The first thing we did was to ask Power to give us something to eat, as we were starving. He said, " If you go to that tree," pointing to it, " you will find some fine corned beef;" and so it turned out. We also found some tea, sugar, and bread in his tent. We threw away the water that was boiling, for fear it might have been poisoned, refilled the " billy," and made some tea. When the black-fellow saw the bread and meat he exclaimed, " Oh, golly, what a feed we shall have !" And so we did. Power tried to eat some breakfast, but complained that we had taken his appetite away. The only money we found in his tent or gunyah consisted of the three five-pound notes with my initials on them.

The spot on which the gunyah was situated was a most commanding position, and it would have been almost impossible to approach it without observation, had Power been awake. It was within half a mile of Quinn's house. I found out afterwards that the signal given by the Quinns when danger was near was the crack of a stock-whip, which meant, "Be on the look-out." The dogs and peacock were also signals, but, as luck would have it, appeared to be off their guard that night.

The place where Power was captured was about fifty miles from the nearest watch-house, and after breakfast we started on our journey. The first difficulty we had to contend with was how the two of us, viz., my brother officer and myself, were to pass these desperadoes at Quinn's house without an attempt at a rescue. The clerk had aroused the Quinns when he had passed to secure the horses, and when we were within sight of the house, we saw six or eight men standing at the door, and the dogs were barking at a great rate, and the peacock shrieking. My brother officer went in advance with Power, revolver in hand, while I remained some distance in the rear armed with Power's double-barrelled gun, so as to protect them if an attempt at a rescue had been made, but no attempt was made, not even a remark while he passed. Of L—— we saw nothing more; after we found the hollow tree he returned to Greta as fast as he could, without, as far as we know, being seen by any one. We mounted Power on the black-fellow's horse until we were able to secure another for him, and at seven o'clock on Sunday night we had him in the Wangaratta lock-up, safe and secure. During the journey he related many of his exploits, and seemed quite proud of his doings. Many of his stories were most amusing, and whenever we met any one on the road he called out, "They have got poor Power at last, but they caught him asleep."

On arriving at Wangaratta, we found the inhabitants were all going to church; in some way it became known that Power was captured, and in a few moments the churches were emptied, and every one flocked to see the notorious bushranger who had kept the whole colony in such a state of excitement for so many months.

It would take me too long to relate one tenth of his anecdotes, nor had I any guarantee as to the truth of them, but I may give one or two for a sample. He stated that he had robbed a number of stores and draymen, at Bright. The morning before he committed the robbery he changed his clothes, putting on very old ones, and mounted a miserable old roan horse which he had picked up for the occasion, leaving his own horse and clothes in some secure place in the bush. After committing the robberies, he started off to his retreat in the mountains, riding in the most unfrequented passes. About sunset in the evening, he met three young men who appeared to him like office lads, or bank clerks; each of them had a revolver round his waist. They came up to him, and said, "Have you seen a man riding a roan horse?" at the same time describing the dress Power had worn in the morning. He replied, "No; who is he?" The young men replied, "We are looking for Power the bushranger, who has stuck up a number of drays and stores near Bright this morning." Power then told them he had seen no one answering the description they gave. Power asked them where they intended spending the night; they said they were going towards Myrtleford; he said he was going in that direction also, and would accompany them in their search for Power. They rode along talking about the robberies, the three young fellows never dreaming they were talking to Power.

After they had gone some distance, Power got them in a certain position, and ordered them to hold up their hands on pain of being shot, at the same time pointing his revolver at them and informing them he was Power the bushranger. He made them all dismount from their horses, undo the belts of their revolvers, let them drop on the road, and move away from them. He then ordered them all to undress and place their clothes on a log, even down to their shirts, and ordering them away from the log, lit a fire and burnt every article! He let their horses go, and then told them they might return to Bright, and inform their employers they had seen Power! I never could ascertain whether this story was true, beyond the fact of his having stuck up the stores and draymen on that road.

Another story Power told me is worth recording. He said he had stuck up a number of draymen on the road between Avenel and Seymour, and after stopping some eight or nine of them and seeing another approach him, he stepped from behind a tree, and ordered the driver to "bail up," calling out, "I am Power, the bushranger," at the same time covering him with his double-barrelled gun. The drayman pulled up his horses, and Power demanded his money, but the driver, who proved himself to be a Scotchman, most positively declined to hand it over. He said, "I have worked hard for my money, and have only £9 upon me, and nothing in the world will induce me to give it up." Power replied, "You see all these gentlemen here," pointing to the drivers of the other waggons, "have given me up all their money, and you will have to do the same." The drayman still remained obdurate, and Power then said to him, " Look here my good man, you see the position I am in; if I allow you to pass without giving me your money, my occupation will be gone. I am a bushranger, and make my living as a highwayman. Suppose I let you pass, the next person I stick up will also refuse to hand over his money, and the public will say I am afraid to shoot a man. I will therefore give you five minutes to think over the matter, and if after that time you still refuse, I will have to shoot you." Power said to me, "I did not want to shoot the poor fellow, so I left him and went behind a tree and prayed to God to soften his heart, and the Lord answered my prayer. At the end of the appointed time, I again called on the drayman to hand over his cash, and he handed it to me without a murmur."

Power was a most careful man in his dress. No one would have thought he was a bushranger, his clothes were always so clean and neat, and he always rode splendid horses (of course, stolen property). After his capture I was a good deal with him. I drove him to Beechworth in my buggy, and he talked all the way; and subsequently I was asked by Captain Standish to bring him from Beechworth to Melbourne by coach, and all the way down he related his adventures and experiences since his escape from Pentridge. On his arrival in Melbourne by the coach, which carried the mails, we stopped at the post-office, where a large crowd awaited his arrival. He put his head out of the coach window and took off his hat to the people, and then, when the coach arrived at Cobb's office, he wanted to make a speech to the crowd, but I prevented his doing so.

On the way from Beechworth after the sentence was passed, he thanked me for all my kindness towards him, and told me he would like to make me a present of a magnificent black mare he had in the mountains (telling me where she was). I asked him how she came into his possession, but he replied, "You must not ask me that question." I said, "Did you get her on the square?" His reply was "No." "Then I can have nothing to do with her," I replied. He afterwards offered me his pipe, but as I was not a smoker I declined the offer.

Power was put on his trial at Beechworth, charged with highway robbery under arms, which meant sticking up the Myrtleford coach and robbing the passengers. He pleaded guilty to one charge, and was sentenced to fifteen years in Pentridge; he served over fourteen years of this sentence, and was then released. He was afterwards employed as gamekeeper to Sir William Clarke, at Bald Hill Station. I had a conversation with him whilst there. He appeared very dissatisfied at the unexciting life he was leading. He was a hale, strong man even then, very fond of telling his experiences to any one who would listen to him.

Our guide, L——, I never saw again after leaving him at the hollow tree the morning of Power's capture. I had letters from him, and paid the £500 reward promised to him, to a gentleman he named, who paid him portions of the sum as he required it, but he made no good use of the money. He squandered it, and it became known in the district that he had informed against Power, in consequence of his having so much money at his disposal. He was galloping his horse one Sunday after he had drawn the last instalment, and in riding home from the hotel, where he had been drinking heavily, he fell from his horse and broke his neck. Power himself never suspected L——, but thought the Quinns had given information, or, as it is termed, "put him away;" he thought it quite impossible for our party to have passed Quinn's house unobserved.

I might add that afterwards the squatter who had given us £15 to obtain his watch, and through whose instrumentality the capture was made, sent in an application to the Government to refund the amount, but the Chief Secretary point blank refused the request.

CHAPTER IV.

A Sporting Party on the Murray—" Winkle "—How to take Aim—After the Ducks—A Night with the Snakes—Kangarooing—A Runaway Bed.

PERHAPS as a change from the somewhat lurid record of crime, which from the very nature of things must constitute the principal portion of a police officer's reminiscences, I may be allowed to turn to the lighter incidents of a sportsman's recreations. Sport was a very different thing years ago, before the progress of settlement had driven the game away from the more readily accessible regions. I can recall many happy days spent on the Murray plains in the exciting chase after the bounding kangaroo, or in dealing devastation among the feathered fowl, which then abounded on the lagoons and swamps along the river's course. For the amusement of my readers I will recall one occasion, which was not without a spice of humorous incident. A party of four, we started from Melbourne for a week's shooting on the Murray river. Three of us were well accustomed to this branch of sport, but the fourth member of the band, a very good fellow, and a valued friend to us all, was better acquainted with legal sharpshooting than with modern arms of precision. Still, he had been seized with a sudden desire to distinguish himself in a new line, and, like Mr. Winkle, was prepared to uphold his reputation. Not owning, and never having owned, a gun, he deputed me to select a weapon, the best breech-loader that money could buy, determined that the birds should not escape, at any rate through any fault of the weapon. I fulfilled the commission accordingly. Intending to camp out most of the time, we laid in a stock of provisions and other necessaries, and, proceeding to Echuca by train, started off to our destination lower down the Murray. We camped the first night at a water-hole near Gunbower, and next morning after breakfast the new gun was brought out to be inspected.

I should state that in all shooting parties it is usual to appoint one of the number as captain. He decides what is to be done each day, and his instructions are law. I was appointed on this occasion. Winkle highly approved of my purchase,

eyeing the gun, nevertheless, as if it were a doubtful point of law, of whose possible consequences he was exceedingly dubious. Another member of the party, who dearly loves a practical joke, suggested that the new weapon ought to be tried without delay, and turning to me, with a twinkle in his eye, said—
"Make him fire off the gun at the black shag sitting on that log in the water."

Winkle trembled at the suggestion, never having fired off a double-barrelled gun in his life, but with legal acumen he objected, on the ground that such a weapon should not be desecrated by being turned against an ignoble object like a shag, and said with dignity he would prefer commencing his shooting when he got amongst the game. This plea, however, availed him not. I told him he must obey orders; and accordingly, having put a couple of cartridges into the gun, I handed the weapon to its owner, who received the gift with manifest consternation. Still he obeyed. First he fixed his eyes steadfastly on the shag, then firmly closed them, and, without taking aim, levelled his weapon, and pulled the trigger. As might have been expected under such conditions, the shot struck the water thirty or forty yards from the bird, which soared away with contemptuous deliberation.

"What on earth do you mean by shooting in that way?" called out our humorous friend.

"What do I mean?" repeated the sporting novice with astonishment.

"Why, you never took aim at the bird," was the reply.

"No," responded Winkle, with virtuous surprise. "Why should I? I have often heard Hare say, and also many other sportsmen, that they never aimed at a bird; they merely looked at it, and pulled the trigger." The retort was evidently considered a crushing negative, though any sportsman will understand the difference between firing off the gun without covering the bird, and pulling the trigger, and not letting the gun follow the eye.

We went on our journey for some distance. We had two buggies, our waggish friend driving with me, and the novice with the remaining member of the party in the second buggy. I was driving about a quarter of a mile ahead, when we saw a huge snake lying in the road. I drove over it, and broke its back, preventing it from moving. We pulled up our buggy and waited till the others came up. Then, for another bit of fun, I ordered Winkle to get out his gun, put it together himself, and shoot the snake. The order, given with the utmost seriousness of countenance, was received with horror. He objected most strongly, pleading that I knew his antipathy to snakes; besides, he had always heard that where there was one snake there was sure to be another close by, and as the grass was long he begged not to be compelled to get out of the buggy. He was quite unaware that the back of the snake was broken, and that the reptile could not move, though it kept raising its head viciously, and wriggling about in a manner quite sufficient to alarm the uninitiated. My companion, alive to the joke, urged me to insist. At last, with the utmost reluctance, he slowly and with unwilling step reached the ground. I told him to aim at the snake. With trembling caution he raised the gun to his shoulder, keeping the while at a respectful distance from the disabled snake, and then pulled both triggers. Relying on the sporting doctrine that it is quite unnecessary to take aim, he fired at random, and I need hardly say that neither shot went anywhere near the snake. Then he got into the buggy as quickly as he could, afraid apparently that the snake was in eager pursuit.

We laughed, and told him that the snake could do him no harm, as its back was broken. He took the joke good-humouredly, but with more seriousness repeated that he had a horror of snakes, and he begged us not to play any practical jokes of this kind upon him.

That night we reached our destination, and met the then manager of the station, who gave us a good account of the game we were likely to see. My companion and I used to have a shooting trip every year to this station, and the manager was accustomed to reserve all the unmanageable horses he met with during the year for us to break in. Turkey shooting in those days required a good deal of skill in getting near the birds, and we often had a pair of horses which would take a considerable time to yoke up, but would return in the evening tired out and quite broken in. The manager began to tell us what a pair of devils he had for us next morning. We were not dismayed, thinking the more spirit the horses had the better, but our verdant friend did not at all coincide with this view. When he went out shooting, he said, he wanted to shoot, and did not like his attention distracted by the antics of wild, untamed animals. The manager, all hospitality, agreed that he should have a quiet, steady pair.

After a good night's rest, off we started in the direction where the game was to be found. At first Winkle declined to repeat his shooting experiences. He preferred holding the horses, and it was not until the afternoon that we could prevail on him to take his gun and creep along a gully where some ducks were hiding in the reed-beds. He was not used to country life, nor to stalking game, and when we called on him to keep as close to the ground as possible, he put down his head and raised another part of his body to such a height, that we could scarcely wonder the ducks rose in affright over such an extraordinary figure, long before he got within range. He, however, was no whit disappointed. Having been directed to fire he obeyed orders, and though more than 200 yards away he discharged both barrels, and came back much satisfied with himself. He explained that we must have started the ducks, but when we showed him the figure he presented when stalking them, he was not surprised at the birds flying off.

We had a good day's sport, and made up our minds to stay at a deserted hut on the run that night. In those days the snakes were very plentiful on the Murray Flats. This was long before selection took place, and the huts deserted during the winter months were taken possession of by those reptiles.

On being made acquainted with this strange fact in natural history, our friend was strongly averse to anything which would savour of the nature of trespass, and disclaimed any desire to serve a writ of ejectment. The manager, who was with us, said that it would be safer to take refuge in the hut than to camp out, as at that season snakes always travelled by night. When we arrived there we found three old bunks, consisting of four posts driven into the ground with bars across them, and an old bag fastened over them. As old campaigners, my companion, myself, and the overseer took possession of the bunks, leaving the less astute members of the party to lie on the floor. Our friend put on his glasses and took a good survey of the position. "Ah!" he said, "I see what it is, the three old birds have taken possession of the bunks, and we," turning to his companion, "have to lie on the floor." As night came on we made ourselves as comfortable as we could under the circumstances, and turned in early. In the night friend number two called out to the snake-hating Winkle, "Lie quiet, a snake has just crawled over me!" At once a light was struck, but the snake could not be found, but the alarmist, who was a very old bushman, declared he distinctly felt a snake crawl over him.

Next day we had another good day's sport, and saw no end of snakes, and again we started our friend off to stalk another lot of ducks. He positively refused to crawl along on his hands and knees, as he did not care about the snakes pecking at his nose and face, so the same exhibition occurred as the day before, he presenting a figure that I feel sure the game in the district had never before seen. There was the same result, the ducks flew away unharmed. On this occasion he did not fire at them, but coming back to the buggy his gun went off of its own accord. On his return we asked him what he fired at, and he candidly admitted that the gun was responsible and not himself. He stated positively he would never again attempt to fire off a gun, for, said he, "I don't quite know which hammer I am to put my finger on when I put the gun on half-cock." It then appeared he put his thumb on the left hammer, whilst his finger was on the right trigger; consequently, the gun went off. We all recognized that there was a great risk in shooting with our friend, and were glad that he decided to put away his gun, and so avoid bagging bigger game than we had any intention of securing.

We decided to cross the Murray and stay the

night at a station on the opposite bank. We arrived late in the evening, and were disappointed to find the owner absent from home. However, bush fashion, we went up to the house and told the housekeeper we intended staying there for the night. Our friend at once asked the housekeeper whether there were any snakes about. She replied, "I don't think there are many. One was seen on the verandah this morning, and he got under the floor of the house, but a good many were seen some time ago." He did not at all relish the idea of sleeping there that night. After a good dinner we went to bed early, our friend, with due regard to his personal comfort, being given the owner's bed. Two of us were sleeping in the next room, and during the night my friend awoke me and said that he heard groaning in the next apartment, and asked me to see what was the matter. I lighted a candle and went into the room.

Such a sight I never witnessed before or since. There was our snake-haunted friend sitting doubled up on the bed, fully dressed, with gaiters on, and bandages round his wrists and neck. He was groaning as if in great pain.

"What on earth is the matter with you?" said I.

"Oh, Hare! Such a night I never spent before

in my life. The snakes have been running up and down the wall after the mice, and I have been afraid that the mice would run up my legs or arms, and the snakes would follow, so I got up, dressed, and put on my gaiters, and tied handkerchiefs round my wrists."

I could scarcely stand for laughing, and went next door and called in my companion, who, appreciating the humour of the situation, exploded with laughter. Never before having slept in a wooden room with a paper partition, our frightened friend did not know that mice invariably amused themselves running races all night within the paper lining. We explained matters to him, and he undressed and got into bed again.

Next day we intended changing our sport, and having a day's kangaroo hunting—the owner of the station being known all over the district as having the best kangaroo dogs on the Murray. The manager warned our friend against getting into a buggy with me driving, saying that I did not know the danger I ran, galloping across the plains as hard as the horses could go, following the dogs. Under this influence he came to me and said, "Hare, I don't think I care about kangarooing; I won't go out to-day." I told him it was his duty to obey orders, and as I had decided we were all to go out kangarooing, he must come with us. I drove the buggy; the horses played up when starting, and he begged to be allowed to stay at home, but we would not hear of his staying by himself, and at last we made a start. The hounds were sent out in a cart, and at an appointed place we all met. The kangaroos were in hundreds, and a pair of dogs were slipped by a man on horseback when at full gallop. The two buggies and half a dozen station hands and blacks, perfectly naked, went in full gallop across the plains, the kangaroos running in every direction, one hound following one kangaroo, and the other another; such a helter-skelter was never before seen. Our friend was perfectly quiet and resigned to his fate. The game took to a clump of timber, and I saw my way to dash through it. The manager, who galloped past us, called out that it was perfect madness to allow me to drive as I was doing. However, I got through all right, but was pulled up on the other side by a deep ravine. Then my friend begged me to stop, and said he did not see anything in kangaroo hunting, and he preferred shooting ducks. We had another run, but he still declared that as far as he was concerned he could see no sport in kangarooing, and he had seen enough to last him his life.

We stayed another night at the station, and the next night crossed the Murray, and went back to Victoria. We had another good day's turkey and duck shooting, and that night we camped on a sand-hill near a shepherd's hut. After selecting a spot whereon to camp, our friend strolled about, and met the wife of the shepherd. He at once entered into conversation with her, and said, " My good woman, are there any snakes about here?" She replied, 'Law, sir, the place is stiff with them. They have been carting in a supply of wood for the winter, and in every hollow log there appears to be a snake." He returned to us downcast and dejected, and taking me aside, said, "Hare, I cannot sleep on the ground to-night; you must let me sleep in the waggon." I consulted with the others, and we agreed, after the miserable nights he had passed, he should be allowed to clear out the waggon, and put his 'possum rug in it. I must describe the position we selected for our camp. It was a steep hill on the side we were on, with a wide creek at the foot of it. His attention was drawn to the position, and we pointed out the possibility of the waggon running down the hill; but he took the precaution of putting chocks under the wheels, so as to prevent such an accident. I had no idea at the time of the reason why my waggish friend took so much trouble to point out the position of the waggon. However, I plainly saw the reason afterwards! We had our tea, which consisted of kangaroos' tails boiled in water, with some pepper and salt, which were not by any means palatable, but after a hard day's shooting anything goes down! Having selected our sleeping places round the fire, we all turned in, and our friend getting into the waggon, coiled up in his rug, began to chaff us, and ask us if there were any snakes knocking about. He little thought what was going to take place during the night. We all fell asleep, and later on I was awakened by dreadful screams from the waggon, calling out, "Hare, Hare, the waggon is off down the hill, and I will be drowned." I jumped up, and there saw the wag of the party at the pole of the waggon, pulling it down the hill. I could scarcely stand for laughing. The frightened occupant jumped out, and not seeing the joker at the pole, called out, "Good heavens, what a narrow escape I've had."

Next morning there was a discussion whether we should go back to Melbourne, or continue shooting.

One of the party was for having another day's sport, but the amateur sportsman turned upon him and told him he knew nothing about shooting, and begged us take no notice of what he said, but to make back to the station at once and endeavour to reach Echuca next day. Finally we agreed to do so.

On the road back one of the blacks who was with us started off in a gallop and rescued our little dog from being picked up by a huge eagle-hawk that was pouncing down upon the spaniel running ahead of us. These eagles, when hungry, generally hunt together, and have often been seen following a large kangaroo until it could scarcely stand; then they would attack it, and tear it to pieces and eat it. We got back to Echuca that night in time to catch the train. Our bag consisted of thirty-five turkeys, 120 couple of ducks, fifty geese, and no end of kangaroo tails. Our friend gave me his gun to sell, and I believe he has never since fired off a shot, and never intends to do so again. He got back to the bosom of his family, and registered a vow that he would never again go for a shooting trip as long as he lived, as he found he was not a sportsman, although highly thought of in his profession.

CHAPTER V.

The Kelly Gang—Ned and Dan Kelly—Steve Hart—Joe Byrne—The Origin of the Bushranging Outbreak—Search Party organized—Murder of Kennedy—M'Intyre's Escape —Arming the Police—Tracking the Gang—Close on them.

THE events in connection with the outbreak of the Kelly gang, from the murder of the ill-fated party of police in the Wombat Ranges, in October 1878, until the capture and death of the bushrangers at Glenrowan, in June 1880, are still too fresh in the minds of the public to need more than the briefest recapitulation as an introduction to my own experiences in their pursuit. Perhaps there was no one who had a better opportunity of obtaining information concerning their career than myself. Not that I wish to take any special credit, but I am merely mentioning facts that came to my knowledge and experiences during the search for the outlaws. For nearly ten months I was engaged searching for them, and both before I went to the north-eastern district and after I was relieved, Captain Standish, the Chief Commissioner of Police, consulted me concerning all the information that came to hand.

Ned Kelly, the leader of the gang, was born in 1854, at Wallan Wallan. At an early age he took to criminal courses, and was regarded as a horse and cattle stealer from his earliest boyhood. He was known to steal carriers' horses at night, "plant" them in the bush until a reward was offered for their recovery, and then in the most innocent manner claim the reward. Afterwards he took to stealing and selling any horses he found straying about. When he was sixteen years of age he joined Power, although he never assisted in any of his sticking-up cases; still, he was with him on two or three occasions when Power committed some of his depredations. He merely took charge of Power's horses at a distance, but he could not be recognized by any of the victims, and consequently he was never tried for any offence in connection with him; but he served two or three sentences for horse and cattle stealing. When with Power, Ned Kelly was a flash, ill-looking young blackguard. He told me the reason he left him was because Power had such an ungovernable temper that he thought Power would shoot him. He told me that when they were riding in the mountains, Power swore at him to such an extent, without his giving him any provocation, that he put spurs to his horse and galloped away home. It was generally supposed by the public that Ned Kelly gave the police some information which led to Power's arrest; but this is entirely untrue. Power would not at that time have trusted Kelly with the knowledge of his whereabouts. Power had a very poor opinion of Kelly's courage, and told me that once or twice Ned Kelly suggested that they should surrender, more especially when Kelly and he were trying to steal some of Dr. Rowe's horses at Mount Battery station, Mansfield, and Dr. Rowe fired on them with a long distance rifle. Power said Kelly turned deadly white, and wished to surrender. He had the greatest difficulty in getting him off the ground, he was in such a fright. Between the interval of his exploits with Power, and the time of the outbreak of the gang of which he was the leader, Ned Kelly had grown into a man, and had become so hardened in crime as to be perfectly reckless.

Ned Kelly had two brothers and four sisters, Dan, Jim, Mrs. Gunn, Mrs. Skillian, Kate and Grace. His father, who died in 1865, was a notorious

DAN KELLY.

criminal, having been transported from Ireland. He married a Miss Quinn, and all her people were thieves. The mother (Mrs. Kelly) is still alive, but was in gaol during most of the time her sons were outlaws, having been convicted of aiding in the shooting of Constable Fitzpatrick.

Dan Kelly was born in 1861, and was a good deal mixed up with Ned in his criminal pursuits. They were the terror of all persons who travelled with stock in that part of the district, and many drovers were accustomed to go miles out of their way to avoid Greta, for fear of their cattle being stolen. Dan was always known to be a cunning low little sneak, he would be prowling about half the night seeing what he could pick up; of course he knew every road, lane, and mountain gully in the district, and could ride about the darkest night and find his way as if in his own garden.

Steve Hart was born in 1860, near Wangaratta, he also was a horse-stealer, and was frequently prowling about of a night to pick up a stray drayman's horse, or any other animal that did not belong to him.

Joe Byrne was born in 1857 at Woolshed, near Beechworth. He was a fine strapping young fellow, but he took early in life to evil courses, and received a sentence of six months in Beechworth for cattle-stealing. He was educated at the Eldorado school, where he and Aaron Sherritt were most intimate friends.

Aaron Sherritt, who figures conspicuously throughout this narrative, was born near Beechworth. His parents and sisters were respectable and well-conducted people, his father having been in the police force in the old country. He was a strapping, tall, well-made young fellow, and associated himself with the Kellys and Byrne in their horse-stealing raids, giving himself up entirely to a disreputable life.

It will be observed that as the Kelly family lived near Greta, the Hart family near Wangaratta, with the Warby ranges behind them, and Joe Byrne's family resided at Woolshed, they had miles of ranges to retreat into with which they were well acquainted, and to this fact I attribute in a great measure their successful evasion from arrest. If, for instance, the police made up their minds to search the interminable ranges at the back of Greta, extending for over one hundred miles, the outlaws would, through their sisters, get the information furnished to them that the police were in that district, and they would shift their position during the night to the Warby Ranges, at the back of Hart's place; if parties of police were sent there, they would move over to Byrne's friends. In this manner they could find retreats over hundreds of miles of impenetrable mountains, amongst which they had been brought up all their lives, and where they knew every road, gully, and hiding-place.

The origin of the bushranging outbreak was the shooting at a young constable named Fitzpatrick in April 1878. He had been sent to arrest Dan Kelly at his mother's house near Greta. He was invited into Mrs. Kelly's hut and there set on by a number of people, and in the scuffle Ned Kelly shot him in the wrist. Mrs. Kelly, the mother of Ned and Dan, with two or three others, was subsequently arrested, tried, and convicted for aiding in the shooting of Fitzpatrick, and received long sentences. Warrants were then issued, and a reward of £100 offered for the arrest of Ned and Dan Kelly. For some months nothing was heard of them; they were doubtless in the district, but the police could not lay their hands on them, although every effort was made to capture them.

In October 1878, search parties were organized of three or four men, and were sent to search the mountains. The party in charge of Sergeant

Kennedy, one of the best men in the force, comprised also Constables Lonergan, Scanlan, and M'Intyre. They had orders to scour the Wombat Ranges. They left Mansfield on the 25th of October, 1878, with pack-horses and provisions to last them some days. Sergeant Kennedy was a shrewd, intelligent man, and there is every reason to believe he had received information of a most positive nature as to where the Kellys were to be found, the information being supplied by a man whom I must call P——, a well-educated fellow, who had held various responsible positions in the district, on the promise from Kennedy that if he arrested the offenders, the reward offered by the Government for their apprehension should be paid to him. It is also stated, that no sooner had P—— given this information to Kennedy and seen the police started in search of the bushrangers, than he went straight to the Kellys and told them that Kennedy was to camp in a certain spot in the Wombat Ranges. Kennedy never for a moment thought the Kellys would attack him; such an idea never entered his head, and he camped for the night in a spot he had selected in the Stringy Bark Ranges, about twenty miles from Mansfield; the country was almost impassable from the impenetrable scrub.

THE CAMP SURPRISED.

The following morning Kennedy and Scanlan got their horses and started off to search the ranges, leaving M'Intyre and Lonergan in the camp; the former was acting as cook for the day. The camp consisted of a tent, which the men slept in. About two o'clock that day the two men left in camp were suddenly called on to "bail up and throw up their hands" by four armed men, who were presenting rifles at them. M'Intyre, being unarmed, immediately obeyed and threw up his hands, his revolver being inside the tent. Lonergan, instead of following the example, ran to get behind the shelter of a tree, at the same time drawing his revolver out of the case, but before he got to the tree he was shot in the forehead, and dropped down dead. The armed men were found to be Ned and Dan Kelly, Joe Byrne, and Steve Hart; they at once took possession of Lonergan's arms and all the other arms lying about the camp. M'Intyre was made to sit on a log, and he had a good opportunity of seeing the faces of the four men. Either Ned or Dan Kelly shot Lonergan, and M'Intyre states that Byrne and Hart were dreadfully cut up at the turn things had taken, especially Byrne, who was nervous and downcast.

The bushrangers were evidently aware that Kennedy and Scanlan were away, and would shortly be returning. They arranged that M'Intyre would sit in some conspicuous place where he could be seen by his comrades, and they themselves laid down in some sheltered spot where they could not be seen, and they advised M'Intyre to induce Kennedy and Scanlan to surrender, saying that if they consented they would not be shot. M'Intyre told Kelly that he would induce his comrades to surrender, if he promised to keep his word.

Kennedy and Scanlan rode into the camp. M'Intyre went forward and said, " Sergeant, I think you had better dismount and surrender, as we have been captured." Kelly at the same time called out, "Put up your hands." They both appear to have grasped the situation in a moment, for Scanlan threw himself from his horse to get behind a tree, but was shot before he reached the ground. Kennedy jumped from his horse, and getting the animal between him and the bushrangers, opened fire upon them. The horse bolted and passed close by M'Intyre, who vaulted on it and galloped off, throwing himself on the horse's neck. Several shots were fired, but, fortunately, none hit him, and he rode off as hard as he could. Kennedy was left then to fight these four scoundrels.

What happened no one knows, beyond what Ned Kelly stated himself. He said that Kennedy was a brave man, and fought the four of them until he had fired all the shots in his revolver. His body was afterwards found a quarter of a mile from where M'Intyre last saw him, with several bullet wounds and fearfully mutilated. Ned Kelly said that after Kennedy was wounded and fell, they all ran up to him, and Kennedy begged them to spare his life for the sake of his wife and children, but the inhuman brute said that he did not like to leave him in the bush in such a state, and so out of compassion he blew his brains out. An inquest was held on the bodies of the murdered men. Lonergan had received seven bullet wounds, one of them through the eye-ball. Scanlan's body had four shot marks on it, the fatal bullet had gone through his lungs. Kennedy's body was fearfully mutilated, he had three bullets through his head, and several in his body. Aaron Sherritt afterwards gave me another version of this matter. He said Ned Kelly told him that he made both Joe Byrne and Steve Hart fire into Kennedy whilst he was lying wounded, as neither of them had shot either Scanlan or Lonergan, and he made them kill Kennedy so as to prevent their turning informers against him and his brother. In support of this theory, it may be noted that when Kennedy's body was found, it was apparent that the bullets which put an end to his life must have been fired by men standing close over him, as the skin was burnt by the powder.

M'Intyre after his escape rode off as fast as the nature of the country would permit, until his horse fell and threw him across a log, on his loins, and then bolted off. M'Intyre felt sure he was being followed by one of the gang, and no doubt they did endeavour to overtake him, but the country was so dense with scrub that they were unable to follow on his tracks. After being thrown from his horse, he ran as far as he could, until through exhaustion he fell down, and close by he found a wombat hole, into which he crept, hoping to evade his pursuers. Whilst he was in this hole in the earth, he tore a sheet out of his pocket-book and wrote as concise an account as he could, thinking if the Kellys did overtake him, he would leave the slip of paper in the hole, in the hope that it might be found some day. Fortunately darkness came on, and M'Intyre got out of the hole and travelled all night on foot. Towards morning he found himself near Mr. Tolmie's station, between Mansfield and Benalla. At first he was rejoiced at seeing some habitation, but to his horror he fancied he saw the police horses which had been ridden by Kennedy's party feeding near the house, and he thought the bushrangers had come down and taken possession of the place. Acting on this idea, he made off as fast as he could. He found his way into Mansfield some time during the afternoon.

I afterwards spoke to M'Intyre concerning these horses, and he told me he felt perfectly convinced in his own mind that he saw the horse he had been riding, together with the three others, but it turned out that they were only the station horses. M'Intyre was much blamed for the way he had acted in the affair, but my own idea is, that unless he had been a brave man, he could not have seized the opportunity in the way he did in vaulting on Kennedy's horse as it passed him. He was of no use to Kennedy, he had no arms in his possession, and the fact of his bolting off as he did, gave Kennedy a better opportunity of shooting one or two of the bushrangers if they attempted to pursue him. He had seen his two companions shot dead and the third fired at; clearly his best course was to escape and give the alarm. There can be no question that if M'Intyre had also been shot (which he would have been, had he not escaped), the world would never have known the fate of the four men. The bush near the spot where the tragedy took place is so dense that, if the bodies had been burned and the ashes covered up, no sign of the bodies could have been discovered.

To show how difficult it was to find anything in the locality, it may be mentioned that poor Kennedy's body, although only a quarter of a mile away from the others, was not found for two or three days, although dozens of people were searching. When found, it was covered with a coat, although Lonergan's and Scanlan's bodies were lying in the camp uncovered. Afterwards I asked Sherritt the cause of Kennedy's body being covered, and he said Ned Kelly told him he was the bravest man he had ever heard of, and out of respect he went all the way to the camp, got a cloak, and threw it over the body, and I have not the least doubt that was the case.

M'Intyre having giving the alarm at Mansfield, a party of police were sent out at once to the Wombat, and after much difficulty they reached the spot described by M'Intyre, and found the two bodies, and some days afterwards the remains of Kennedy were found as stated. The bodies had to be tied on horseback to be brought out of the forest, and they were buried at Mansfield, where a monument has been erected to the memory of the murdered men. Kennedy was a great favourite with every one. He left a wife and children at Mansfield. The Government behaved liberally, allowing the widow to draw her husband's full pay to support herself and children ever since.

The news of these murders was very soon sent to all parts of the colonies, and caused great consternation. Captain Standish at once despatched the inspecting superintendent to the district, and mounted constables from all parts of the colony were sent in pursuit of the offenders. The police were blamed for being unprepared for such an outbreak, but, to my certain knowledge, for years Captain Standish had been asking for authority to arm his men with proper carbines, but his request was refused, the men not even being supplied with ammunition to practise with, because of the expense. Yet when this outbreak took place, blame was heaped upon the head of the department for being in such a state of unpreparedness. Authority was then given to purchase arms that were thought suitable for the purpose, but rifles of the description required could not be obtained. The military sent some old-fashioned rifles, but they were not to be depended on. Captain Standish then obtained authority to purchase from a gun-maker in Melbourne a large number of shot-guns, breech-loaders, and these were sent to the north-eastern district, and were well adapted for the purpose, and the men felt great confidence in using them. Each of these breech-loading shot-guns cost the Government about £8. However, we had to purchase some reliable weapons, and these shot-guns were considered the best, especially for inexperienced men.

The inspecting superintendent, and the officer in charge of the district, at once set to work to organize search parties to go in pursuit of the gang. The whole district at this time was in an intense state of excitement, and reports came from all parts of the district that suspicious persons answering the description of the bushrangers had been seen. There were several hundred square miles of country which the murderers knew every inch of, and it was difficult to say in which direction they would fly. One of the parties organized to search for the offenders found, within a few miles of the spot where the murders were committed, a very strong stockade, built of logs laid one on top of the other, with loop-holes all round, through which shots could be fired, and the person firing remain quite unseen, the trees within one hundred and fifty yards being full of bullet marks, where evidently considerable practice had taken place. It is believed that the bushrangers were living in this stockade when they attacked Kennedy's party, and from all appearances had been living there for some considerable time.

Aaron Sherritt told me it was quite by accident that Joe Byrne and Hart happened to be with the Kellys when they attacked the police. They were always great friends and companions in their horse-stealing raids, and Sherritt said they had no idea of shooting the police the morning they started to attack the camp. Their chief aim was to secure some good fire-arms and horses, and they were under the impression that all they would have to do was to cover them with their rifles, and the police would surrender. Instead of this they had to shoot the police to save their own lives.

Of course the bushrangers took away everything belonging to the murdered men. The police had good Webley revolvers, a Spencer carbine, and two shot-guns, the latter borrowed from some one at Mansfield. The police horses were also taken away by the gang.

The Government immediately offered a reward of £1000 for information that would lead to the apprehension of the offenders, they were outlawed, and every inducement was given to people to inform against them. After the murders the first information that was received concerning them was from the Murray River, below Wodonga, about ninety miles from the scene of the murder. They called at the house of a German, who knew them. They were riding the police horses belonging to Kennedy's party, and had their arms in their possession, and were seen going towards the Murray. They evidently meant to cross the river, but it was flooded, and they got on some of the islands and were very nearly drowned. The police had information of this, but they either disbelieved it, or failed to take action. At all events, a day or two afterwards the outlaws were seen making their way back riding through the water, and obliged to swim their horses to get out. When they reached the shore they had to make a fire to dry their arms, and they remained there some hours.

The next thing heard of them was their going through Wangaratta about daylight, crossing the bridge through the town, the whole country being flooded to such an extent that they were compelled to come through the town. Four men were seen crossing under a culvert on the railway, and it was known that no one but persons who

AN OPPORTUNITY MISSED. 109

had resided in Wangaratta could have known how to cross the creek in the swollen state it was in, as there was great risk in doing so. Information was given to the police at Wangaratta, but they doubted the truth of the report. After a day or two convincing proof was given that the four men seen passing under the railway were the bushrangers. An effort was then made to follow their tracks. This could be done by the men in full gallop, as the country was so boggy the tracks were plainly visible. The police tracked the foot-prints of the outlaws' horses to a well-known sympathizer's house, where it was afterwards ascertained the outlaws had breakfasted. Then the tracks were followed up still further into the Warby Ranges, and the police found Kennedy's horse, which the outlaws had abandoned. The animal was knocked up and its feet were bleeding from travelling over stones without shoes.

This I consider the best opportunity thrown away of capturing the offenders throughout the whole of the search. But unfortunately there was an officer at that time stationed at Wangaratta who was from physical and other disqualifications quite unfit to be sent on duty of this kind. Instead of following up the tracks when he found the lame

110 THE LAST OF THE BUSHRANGERS.

and bleeding horse with signs of having recently been ridden, he threw up the search and made all his men return back to Wangaratta to show he had found the horse. It was afterwards discovered that the outlaws at this time were completely done up; their horses had been some days without feed, and they themselves were wet and tired out. There would have been no difficulty in capturing them. Unfortunately the inspecting superintendent was engaged in some other part of the district, and so also was the officer in charge of the district. The outlaws had got back to near where their relations lived. They had the Kellys' house on one side of them, and the Harts' on the other, and they could go to their own blood relations for any food and help they required.

Search parties were kept up all over the district, men sleeping out, or I should say staying out without fire or shelter; badly-fed horses knocked up, reports coming in from every direction hundreds of miles off, that the Kellys had been seen here, there, and everywhere. Many of these reports were circulated for the purpose of deceiving the police. The inspecting superintendent had had a great deal of experience in the detective force, and was able to obtain information from persons that no one else would think of getting it from. He set to work to endeavour to organize men of this class and get information as to the whereabouts of the outlaws, but there was the greatest difficulty in doing this. The murders committed by the outlaws had created such a scare in the district, that any person who did know anything of their movements was afraid to say anything about it; besides which, they had such a crowd of relations in the district, that it was impossible to find a person who was not in some way or other interested or connected with the gang. No one but the police themselves knew the hardships they went through all that winter whilst searching for the outlaws. They did it most cheerfully, one and all. Their whole aim and object was to fall in with the Kellys. The officers had a most trying time. They had to decide between false and deceiving reports, and those that were true. They were constantly on the move themselves, meeting persons in the bush quite alone, and obtaining information concerning the outlaws, some purposely misleading with a view of favouring the outlaws and getting payment for their services.

CHAPTER VI.

Euroa Bank Robbery—Euroa—"Sticking up" Mr. Younghusband's Station—Mr. Macauley "bailed up"—The Hawker Gloster—Cheap Outfits—The Raid on the Bank—The Manager and Family made Prisoners—The Return to Mr. Younghusband's—The Retreat of the Gang and Liberation of the Prisoners—Explanatory Statement of the Author.

THE next exploit of the gang was the Euroa Bank robbery, on the 11th Dec. 1878. Euroa is situated on the main railway line between Melbourne and Sydney, about one hundred miles from the former. The town at that time had about three hundred inhabitants; there was a police station, where one mounted man was stationed, and it had two hotels and some substantially built buildings in it. A court was held there once a month, and the town was built close by the railway line. The bank that was stuck up was within fifty or sixty yards of the railway station, and trains are constantly passing throughout the day; the nearest townships

AT MR. YOUNGHUSBAND'S. 113

on each side of Euroa are Lowground on the Melbourne side, about nine miles distant, and Violet Town on the north side, about eleven miles. A considerable amount of business is, however, done in this place. It is the outlet for a large agricultural district, reaching down the valley of the Goulbourne river; at the back of it, and but a short distance away, are the Strathbogie ranges, which are covered with thick scrub, and heavily timbered for thirty or forty miles, reaching to near Mansfield, giving excellent cover for any persons trying to escape justice.

About noon on Monday, the 18th of December 1878, an *employé* named Fitzgerald, on Mr. Younghusband's station, was sitting in the hut eating his dinner, when a man who looked like an ordinary bushman quietly sauntered up to the door, and taking his pipe out of his mouth inquired if the manager, Mr. Macauley, was about. Fitzgerald replied, "No, but he will be back towards evening. Is it anything in particular? Perhaps I will do as well." The bushman said, "No, never mind; it is of no consequence," and then walked away from the hut. Fitzgerald continued eating his dinner without taking any further notice of the man; but he happened to look up, and saw the bushman beckoning

I

to some person in the distance. About five minutes afterwards, two more rough-looking characters joined the bushman; they were leading four very fine horses, in splendid condition, they were three bays and a gray. The three men went to the homestead, which was close to the hut, and walked in. They met Mrs. Fitzgerald, the wife of the *employé* already mentioned, who was engaged in some household duties.

The old dame was considerably surprised at the strangers walking in without an invitation, and asked them who they were, and what they wanted. One replied, "I am Ned Kelly, but you have nothing to fear from us, we shall do you no harm; but you will have to give us some refreshment, and also food for our horses. That is all we want." The old lady was naturally very much surprised, and called out to her husband to come to her. Fitzgerald left his dinner at the hut, and walked over to the house, when his wife introduced him to the strangers, saying, "There is Mr. Kelly, he wants some refreshments, and food for his horses." By this time Kelly had drawn his revolver, evidently to show them there was no joking on his part; and Fitzgerald, no doubt thinking discretion the better part of valour, accepted the inevitable, and resignedly said, " Well, if the gentlemen want any refreshment, they must have it."

Shortly after this conversation had taken place, the station hands began to drop in for their dinner. Joe Byrne took up his position outside, keeping watch over the place, and Dan Kelly found the horse-feed, and was attending to the horses. Ned Kelly and Hart, as the men approached the homestead, made prisoners of all of them; Ned took possession of a detached building, which had been used as a store-room, into which he put Fitzgerald, and each man that came up to the station was served in the same manner, and the door locked. The women on the station were in no way interfered with, and they were all assured that no harm was intended to anybody; as each man walked up for his dinner, they were very quietly ordered to "bail up," and were unresistingly marched into the storehouse, no violence being used towards any of them, as they went quietly. Ned Kelly put several questions to each of the workmen, making inquiries about every one on the station, so as to test the credibility of each of them; their answers appeared to satisfy him, he was very quiet in his manner, and kept telling the men they had nothing to fear, provided they did not interfere with him or his companions.

About five o'clock in the afternoon Mr. Macauley, the manager of the station, rode up to the homestead (he had been to one of the out-stations), and when crossing the creek which led up to the station he noticed, with some surprise, the quietness which reigned about the place, and the absence of the station hands about the huts. However, he did not give it a second thought, and proceeded on his way, until nearing the storehouse, when he suddenly reined up. This was in consequence of Fitzgerald calling out to him from the building, "The Kellys are here, you will have to bail up." He could not believe this at first, but almost at that instant Ned Kelly came out of the house, and covering him with his revolvers, ordered him to "bail up." Macauley without dismounting said, "What is the good of your sticking up the station? We have got no better horses than those you have." Ned Kelly replied, "We are not going to take anything, we only want some food, and rest for our horses, and sleep for ourselves."

Macauley, seeing it was no use offering any resistance, at once dismounted, and surrendered. They did not treat him as they did the others, but allowed him to remain at liberty for some time, but always keeping a watchful eye upon him. Even then Macauley did not believe they were the Kelly gang, but when Dan Kelly came out of the house, he recognized, as he said, "his ugly face" from the photos he had seen of him. Macauley said, "Well, as we are to remain here, we may as well make ourselves as comfortable as possible, and have our tea." The outlaws however were too cautious, and only two of them sat down together, whilst the others kept a look-out, and then they relieved each other. They also took great care that some of their prisoners should taste the food first, being apparently afraid of poison being put in.

About this time a hawker named Gloster, who had a shop at Seymour, but was in the habit of travelling about the country with a general assortment of clothing and fancy goods, drove his waggon up to the entrance of the station, and according to his usual custom unharnessed his horses, and made preparations for camping out for the night; and having made all in readiness, he walked up to the station to get some water to make his tea with. When he reached the hut, he was told "the Kellys" were there, and that he would have to "bail up." Macauley, knowing Gloster to be a plucky fellow, was afraid that he might draw his revolver and there would be blood shed; however, Gloster got his water from the kitchen, and was going back to his cart, when Ned Kelly called out to him to stop. Gloster turned round and looked at him, but thinking it was all a lark, went on his way towards his cart. Dan Kelly immediately raised his gun, and was about to fire, when Ned Kelly ordered him not to do so. Macauley called out to him to "bail up," in order to prevent bloodshed. Gloster, who appeared a very obstinate fellow, took no notice of the threats of the Kellys, or the entreaties of Macauley, but steadily continued on his way and got up into his cart. Ned Kelly appeared to be losing his temper, and went down to the cart followed by his brother Dan. Ned then put his revolver to Gloster's cheek, and ordered him to come out of his cart, or he would blow his brains out. Many angry words passed between them, and it was only by the endeavours of Macauley that Ned Kelly was prevented shooting Gloster.

Kelly then said he would let him off this time, at the same time praising his own leniency, by saying not one man in a hundred would have dealt so leniently with him, after the manner in which he had behaved. Dan Kelly was evidently eager for blood, as he expressed a strong wish to put a bullet through "the wretch." Gloster was then marched up to the store-room, and locked up with the other prisoners. The four ruffians then proceeded to ransack the hawker's cart, and provide themselves with a new fit out; they made regular bush-dandies of themselves, and helped themselves pretty freely to the contents of the scent-bottles which they found amongst the stock. They also took what fire-arms he had. Before going to bed for the night, the Kellys opened the door of the store-room, and let the prisoners out for a little while to get some fresh air, but at the same time holding their revolvers in their hands and keeping a sharp look-out after them all. The Kellys had frequent conversations with their prisoners in a most friendly manner, and conversed freely on any subject. All night long two of the outlaws kept guard, whilst the others slept. Tuesday morning they were up early; they appeared to keep a good watch on the approaches to the homestead, so that no information would reach Euroa that would interfere with the successful carrying out of their plans of robbing the National Bank.

About two o'clock on Tuesday afternoon a party of four men, named Mr. McDougal, Mr. Dudley, Mr. Casement, and Mr. Jennant, who were returning from the Strathbogie ranges, were "bailed up," and made prisoners. Mr. McDougal's account of what took place is as follows:—" We had just reached the railway gates where there is a crossing to Mr. Younghusband's station, three of us driving in a spring-cart, and Mr. Jennant on horseback. The gates were closed, and nothing was further from our thoughts than the idea of the Kelly gang being close to us; we were laughingly speculating with each other on the chances of the gates, which are on private property, leading into the run, being locked. Mr. Jennant got down from his horse, and finding them unlocked, was opening them, when two men suddenly made their appearance, one coming from behind us on horseback, and the other advancing on foot in front. Both presented revolvers, and called on us to 'bail up.'

"The one on horseback, who, I afterwards learned, was Ned Kelly, cried out, 'Surrender, or you will be shot.' As both men looked like mounted policemen in plain clothes, and held up handcuffs and accused us of stealing the trap we were driving, we at first thought they were troopers, and Mr. Dudley called out, 'What right have you to arrest us?' and appeared as if he was not going to take any notice of their summons. Ned Kelly then rode close up to him, shouted in a violent manner, at the same time presenting a revolver at his head, and said, 'I'll shoot you dead on the spot if you give me any cheek.' Fearing Kelly was going to carry out his threat, I interposed and asked Dudley to surrender quietly, as it was no use resisting, and said to Kelly, ' You would not shoot an old man!' Kelly replied, 'I won't harm the old man if he surrenders quietly.' A tall young man (Byrne) told us to drive up to the homestead. As we approached the gate leading to the station, one of the station hands opened it, and said in a laughing manner, pointing to Ned Kelly and addressing us, 'Gentlemen, allow me to introduce you to Mr. Edward Kelly.' This was the first intimation who our captors were, and the information was by no means a pleasant one, and did not tend to re-assure us; in fact we were all greatly frightened, and for myself I may say my heart was in my mouth. When we got to the store-room we found Dan Kelly and Hart there guarding the place, in which the manager Mr. Macauley and about twenty others had been imprisoned for twenty-six hours.

"The store-room was a wooden building about twenty yards away from the house; it only had one door and window, near each other, and was easily guarded. Our party of four were put into the room with the others, and, there being no ventilation, we soon found the atmosphere very hot and close. In the meantime the gang had thrown everything out of our cart, they took possession of a rifle and double-barrelled gun, eighty bullets, and some powder and caps.

"Our imprisonment lasted eight hours, during which time, however, several of us were permitted to go out occasionally to get some fresh air, but we were never allowed out of sight. Only the men were put in confinement, the women being allowed to walk about, and they were in no way molested, but from some remark I heard dropped by Dan Kelly (who appeared the greatest ruffian of the lot and a thorough type of a larrakin), he did not desire to leave them alone; he said something about having a lark with the women, but was apparently restrained by his brother. During the time we were in the store-room four trains passed, two each way, and when any of these were heard approaching, we were kept close and told not to make any noise."

This statement of Mr. McDougal, almost verbatim as related, was given by him to the reporter of the *Melbourne Argus* on the evening of the day after the occurrence.

The next step taken by the gang, after capturing these men, and openly stating their intention of robbing the bank at Euroa, was, about half-past two o'clock, to destroy the telegraph line, leaving their prisoners guarded by Joe Byrne. They got tomahawks, and cut down one of the telegraph posts, tearing away all the wire for a considerable length, so that it could not be repaired by the usual quantity of wire carried by a line repairer; they cut down the posts on both sides of the line, and scattered the wire in every direction. Whilst doing this, a further capture of four men who were working on the line as gangers, and who saw them cutting down the wires, was made. These men walked towards the bushrangers to ask them what they meant by cutting down the wires, when Ned Kelly called on them to "bail up." They did so, when told who their captors were, without making any resistance, and were at once marched up to the store-room, into which they were put with the rest of the prisoners.

At half-past three o'clock Ned and Dan Kelly, with Steve Hart, started for Euroa, all dressed in new clothes stolen from Gloster the hawker's cart. They plainly stated they were going to rob the National Bank, but before leaving they got a cheque on this bank signed by the manager Mr. Macauley for a small amount, about three pounds. Ned Kelly drove Gloster's cart, with a hood over it. Dan Kelly took McDougal's, and Hart rode one of the horses. They turned their own horses into the paddock before leaving. Joe Byrne, left in charge of the prisoners, was heavily armed, having two revolvers in his belt, a double-barrelled gun in his hand, and two rifles placed within easy reach. He marched round the building whilst all the prisoners were locked in, and was evidently most watchful.

Whilst the three were away from the station a train stopped in front of the door; a man, who proved to be a line repairer, named Watts, jumped down from the train, coming from the north; he had been sent to repair the line, and he evidently saw that it had not been injured by accident. He walked towards the station for assistance, and to ascertain who had caused the break in the line, when he was suddenly pulled up by Byrne and ordered to approach him, and he also was put into the store-room, having been first searched for fire-arms. Byrne asked him several questions as to the movements of the police and their numbers at the adjoining townships. Nothing else of note transpired during the absence of Ned and his companions from the station.

The proceedings of the three outlaws after leaving the station were as follows. It will be remembered the bank was three miles from Younghusband's station, and they left it at half-past three o'clock. These banks as a rule close about this hour, and when the outlaws reached the township the bank door was closed. It was then five minutes to four as Ned Kelly drew up the hawker's cart in front of the bank, sending his brother and Steve Hart to the back of the premises. Ned then knocked at the front-door; one of the clerks asked who was there. Kelly replied, "I have a cheque of Mr. Macauley's to change; will you please cash it?" The clerk answered, "It is after hours, and we cannot open the door now;" but Kelly begged so hard, saying it would be a great inconvenience not to get the cash that night, that the clerk opened the door and admitted him. Ned closed the door after him, and at once presented a revolver at his head, and ordered him to "bail up." At the same time Steve Hart, with a revolver in each hand, entered the back-door, and they took possession of the fire-arms that were in the bank.

Ned Kelly went in search of Mr. Scott the manager, and found him in an office adjoining the bank. He stood at the end of the table, at the same time covering Scott with a revolver, and said, "I am Ned Kelly; bail up." Mr. Scott's revolver was lying at the other end of the table, and had he picked it up, he would have been shot dead on the spot. Scott did not at first throw up his arms, but they pretty soon made him do so. Ned Kelly then went back to the bank, and left Hart in charge of Scott, and ransacked the place, and took possession of all the cash that had been in use during the day, which amounted to between £300 and £400 in notes, gold, and silver.

Kelly next went over the private apartments where Mr. Scott's family and servants were, and Scott cautioned him concerning his behaviour towards them, thereupon Hart at once pointed his revolver at his head, and told him to be careful how he addressed Kelly. Mrs. Scott was not the least alarmed when she found out who her visitors were, and began chaffing Kelly, and telling him he was a much better-looking man than she fancied he would be; but he was most polite towards her, and told her he wanted her with all the family to get ready to take a drive to Mr. Younghusband's station, three miles off. Mrs. Scott at once obeyed his commands, and told all the children and servants to put on their hats, as they were all obliged to go for a drive. Kelly went back into the bank, and told Scott he knew there was more money in the bank, and he insisted upon having it. The accountant opened the safe, and Kelly took £1500 in notes, 300 sovereigns, £90 in silver, and thirty ounces of gold-dust. He then went into the strongroom, but left the bills and securities undisturbed. Kelly often said whilst in the bank, that it was no use resisting them, as he had eight armed men outside the bank, and he could call them to his assistance; but this was only " blow."

Mrs. Scott afterwards told me that when Kelly spoke to her, she could hardly believe he could be the person he represented himself to be; he was a tall, handsome man, well dressed (with the hawker's clothes on), and spoke so kindly to her. She once or twice said, " Oh, nonsense, you are not that bloodthirsty villain you have been represented to be." I might here state, that after the murders at the Wombat, the description of the outlaws was circulated all over the colony, and special measures were taken to protect the banks, and all kinds of weapons were supplied to their officers. It was feared that they would stick up one of these institutions, and Euroa was one of the most likely to be attacked; and yet the ease with which the whole affair was conducted appears to an outsider almost ridiculous.

The gang, having secured all the cash and arms in

the bank, commenced to make preparations for their departure, and return to Mr. Younghusband's station. Provision had to be made for the carting away of the whole household, which consisted of Mr. and Mrs. Scott, two bank clerks, Mrs. Scott's mother, and seven children and two servants. Kelly went to Scott, and said, "You have such a large household, I must have your buggy; go and put your horse in it." Scott refused to do this, saying his groom was out, and told Kelly he had better do it himself. Kelly replied, "Well, I will do it myself." He accordingly harnessed the horse, and put Mrs. Scott and family into the buggy, she driving it; and before starting away Ned Kelly, seeing that Mrs. Scott was so little scared at their presence, said to her, "Now, none of your larks."

He then told Mr. Scott he would have to go with him in the hawker's waggon; but before leaving the bank, Mr. Scott invited the bushrangers to have a drink of whisky with him, which they accepted, making Mr. Scott drink first, for fear of the liquor being drugged. They all drank each other's health. The remainder of the party were divided, and put equally in the three conveyances. The hawker's waggon came first, with Dan Kelly driving, next came Mrs. Scott with her own buggy, and

Ned Kelly drove the other cart, with Steve Hart bringing up the rear on horseback. When driving along, Mr. Scott and Ned Kelly had a long conversation, and he told the bank manager all about the shooting the police at the Wombat, and showed him the gold presentation watch he had taken from Sergeant Kennedy's body, and said, "It was I who shot Constable Lonergan." Scott asked Kelly what Hart would have done to him when he threatened to strike him in the bank; his reply was, "He would have shot you dead on the spot." Whilst travelling along to the station, and when about a quarter of a mile from Euroa, they had to pass the cemetery; they observed a large party of people returning from a funeral, and these people were walking towards the cavalcade.

Ned Kelly took his revolvers from his belt and looked at Mrs. Scott, with a peculiar expression on his face, as much as to say, the first person who gives the alarm will be the first to die. The return funeral party passed them without taking the least notice of them, and so they continued their journey. Mr. Scott asked Kelly which road he intended taking. Kelly replied, "Oh, the country belongs to us, we can go any road we like." Scott asked Kelly to drive, as he knew the road, but he refused this request. The road was very bad, and the cart going up a steep bank upset. Scott ran to the horse's head, and Kelly lifted out one of the servants; they got the cart up and made a fresh start. The money stolen from the bank was lying in the cart which Kelly drove. On arriving at the station, all the males were put in the store-room, and the females and children were allowed to go into the house.

It was then half-past five o'clock. The gang began to make preparations for starting off, when a train was seen approaching from Euroa. It pulled up opposite the station, with the intention of picking up the line repairer Watts, who had been left at this spot an hour or so before. Ned Kelly called out, "Here comes a special train with bobbies, but we are ready for them, we don't care how many there are, we can fight them." The train after waiting a short time moved on; the driver, not seeing Watts anywhere, started for Benalla.

During the absence of the gang at Euroa Mr. McDougal suggested to some of the prisoners to make an effort to escape, as there were fifteen or sixteen axes hanging up in the store; "and," he added, "if each of us takes one, and commences chopping our way out, we can easily manage it." But the whole party declined to assist in their escape, for, said they, "some of us must be shot in the attempt." Besides, it was generally urged that they had nothing to gain by the attempt which would compensate for the great risk, and they were pretty sure to be released when the bushrangers returned from Euroa. Tea was got ready for the women and children, and Mrs. Scott appeared almost to enjoy the situation in which she found herself. The Kellys had their tea also, and then, much to the relief of those in confinement, they saw evident signs of the gang departing. The money taken from the bank was distributed amongst the gang; so also the arms taken from the prisoners and bank officials. Ned Kelly came to the store-room, and announced that they were about leaving, and warned his prisoners they were not to stir for three hours (it was then about half-past eight); he said, "If one of you leaves this spot within three hours I will shoot that man dead. You cannot any of you escape me in this country, I can track you anywhere, and I can assure you I will keep my word." He then called upon Mr. Macauley to come to the front, and he said to him, "I will hold you responsible for the escape of any of these prisoners until the period I have named has expired. Mind! if you let one of them go, I will meet you some time or other, and then you may consider yourself a dead man!" Before leaving, Ned Kelly came to the door of the store-room, and asked Mr. McDougal for his watch. He handed it to him and told him it was a keepsake from his dead mother. Kelly apparently whispered and said, "No, I will never take that from you," and returned it to him, taking, instead, a watch from Mr. Macauley; and Byrne took Mr. Scott's watch from him.

The outlaws then mounted their horses, which were all splendid animals; it was then half-past eight o'clock and quite dark. Hart and Dan Kelly began to ride about, and show off on their horses, and brag about what they were going to do when they met the police. It was noticed by some of the prisoners that, when the gang returned from Euroa with their prisoners, before they came to the house, signals passed between them and Byrne, who was on guard; this was evidently pre-arranged, so as to denote all was well. After the gang left, they rode off in the direction of the Strathbogie ranges, and nothing more was seen of them. The prisoners then began to discuss what had best be done; some were for starting off at once, others thought they would only be risking their lives, and it was feared the outlaws might have left one of their party to watch; so the majority decided it was safer to wait until the three hours were up.

The station hands during their confinement took the matter very easily; they were well fed, and passed away the time chiefly in playing cards, knowing nothing serious was likely to happen to them.

Most of them looked upon the affair as a capital joke, which had cost them nothing but their confinement. At half-past ten o'clock they all agreed it was time to get out, which they had no difficulty in doing. Mr. and Mrs. Scott and party returned at once to Euroa, which they reached at midnight; the rest of the people stopped at the station that night, except Mr. Casement and McDougal, who went to the house of the former, who lived not far from Euroa.

It was noticed by all the prisoners, that during their imprisonment, although they were domineering in giving their orders, no attempt at violence or roughness was used towards any of them. Ned Kelly was the most communicative of the gang, and conversed freely with many of the prisoners during the day, asking questions as to the movements of the police, and talking of the kick-up which they had caused in the force. When Mr. Scott got back to Euroa at midnight, the bank was just in the same state as when he had left it— the doors all locked, and the inhabitants of the township perfectly unconscious of what had happened in the midst of them during the afternoon. Some of my readers in England may possibly not be able to grasp the matter in its true light. A few remarks in explanation of the doings of the outlaws may therefore not be out of place.

It was evident the gang knew perfectly well the ways and doings of the bank, the hour of closing, and who the occupants were. They wanted a base of operations, where they could confine any one who happened to see them, so that no information might be given concerning them. They selected Younghusband's station, which from its position was well adapted for their purpose. They wanted food for their horses, and rest for themselves, as they would probably have to ride day and night before they reached their mountain retreat. They knew the police would endeavour to follow their tracks, and they had to keep on the alert. But every pass and track in the mountains was known, and every hiding-place familiar to the gang. After an exploit of this kind they seldom rode together. Each man took his own line to the first of several appointed meeting-places. If something occurred to prevent any one of them from putting in an appearance there, they made for the second, and so on until they met. When robbing the bank, they fixed on a time when they knew it would be closed, and they could remain inside without raising any suspicion. Fortune favoured them in a marvellous manner. The hawker, coming to Younghusband's, gave them an opportunity of dressing themselves so respectably, that no one meeting them would take them to be

SYMPATHIZERS. 135

bushrangers; the carts also were of great use to them, and they could scarcely have carried out their plans without them. No doubt all the prisoners who were put into the store-room will be looked upon as cowards, but it should be remembered that it was a well-known fact that, after the Wombat murders, the gang were only too anxious to shed blood, especially Dan Kelly, who was the most bloodthirsty of the lot, and on the least provocation would have done so, his brother frequently having to restrain him from shooting any one he met in the bush.

The prisoners were all taken by surprise. Although they may have had fire-arms near them, the moment they attempted to touch them they would have been shot dead on the spot. Besides, in the store-room the gang had several of their sympathizers who were put amongst the prisoners, so that they could give intelligence by signs to the outlaws, should a rush have been contemplated; the sympathizers were not known to the others in confinement. People in the bush, or on stations, seldom or never carry fire-arms; they have no money about them to lose, and know the bushrangers will not harm them. They do not suspect every one they meet to be a bushranger, especially fine, good-looking, and well-dressed men, as Ned Kelly and Joe Byrne were. There is no doubt the gang had great luck all that day. Their plans were well laid, and carried out splendidly. They never molested the working men or farmers, and in that way gained great sympathy amongst all classes of people, and information concerning the outlaws was withheld from the police. I have often spoken to respectable farmers, and pointed out to them that it was their duty to assist the police, and their reply was, " I want to stand aloof from everything connected with the Kellys; if they hear the police have been to my place, my stacks will be burnt down, my fences broken, and probably all my cattle and horses will be stolen." The only policeman in Euroa on the day of the robbery was absent from his station on some other duty, but had he been in barracks, he would probably not have heard of the matter until twelve o'clock at night. At daylight the police attempted to pick up the tracks of the outlaws. There were foot-prints of horses leading in every direction. The sympathizers who had been in confinement up to eleven o'clock that night, had mounted their horses, and kept riding round the station in every direction, together with the scouts who had been watching all day, one starting off in one direction and another in an opposite one, under the pretence of looking for the tracks of the offenders, whereas it was for the sole purpose of baffling the trackers when daylight came.

CHAPTER VII.

The Police at Euroa—Aaron Sherritt—Jerilderie—Capture of the Police Station and Constables—Amateur Policemen—The Royal Hotel stuck up—Raid on the Bank of New South Wales—£2000 taken—Kelly's Autobiography—His Account of the Fitzpatrick Affair—Departure of the Gang—Return to their Haunts.

VERY shortly before the Euroa Bank robbery, news came to hand that the outlaws were about to make an attempt to leave Victoria, and cross the Murray into New South Wales. The description of the place of crossing and other details were given in such a circumstantial manner, that it convinced both the inspecting superintendent and the officer in charge of the district that the Kellys were to cross the Murray on the night of the 9th December 1878. The inspecting superintendent went to Albury, and he had hardly arrived there when he received a telegram, stating that the bank at Euroa had been stuck up by the outlaws. He immediately took a special train to Euroa. Before the arrival of the inspecting superintendent a party of police were on the ground, and were waiting for daylight in order to find which direction the outlaws had taken. The police had some black trackers with them, but these were of little use, being Victorian blacks, whose sense of sight and sagacity had been destroyed by drink. All day long search was made, but no trace of the outlaws could be obtained. The police were sent in every direction, trying to find out some tidings of the outlaws, but without effect. Some of the men were so knocked up from want of sleep, and the heat, that it was thought many of them would have to go into hospital. The inspecting superintendent was also exhausted with the hardships he had gone through, and was suffering from bad eyes to such an extent, that Captain Standish had to relieve him.

The day after the Bank robbery took place Captain Standish started for Euroa. When he got there he found the inspecting superintendent so ill that he telegraphed for me to come up and take his place, ordering me to report myself at Euroa that evening. I did so. On my arrival I heard the statements concerning the robbery, and endeavoured to obtain all the information about the outlaws I could possibly gather. The whole community were perfectly scared at what had taken place, and rumours were coming in from all quarters concerning persons being seen answering the descriptions of the outlaws.

When the bushrangers appeared at Euroa they were riding three bay horses and one grey. Every report that came to hand had to be inquired into and reported on, otherwise complaints were made that the police took no notice of information furnished to them. The most absurd statements were made, too ridiculous to be noticed. For instance, a squatter sent in word to Benalla that the Kelly gang were shooting parrots near his garden. The messenger who conveyed the information was told to go and inform the police as fast as his horse could carry him. The officer in charge of the district sent the messenger back, and told him to tell his master that he must be mad to send in such an absurd message. The officer sent a constable to inquire who the people were that were shooting birds, and found them to be a survey party. The squatter was under the impression that no inquiries were made concerning his report, and afterwards wished to bring a charge against the officer for not capturing the Kellys when he had sent word to him where they were to be found, and to this day he believes that if steps had been taken on that occasion the outlaws would then have been arrested.

On another occasion a message was wired one Sunday morning to Melbourne to the late Chief Justice, that the gang had been in Mrs. Rowe's garden cutting cabbages, near Euroa, and similar reports were daily being made, all of which had to be inquired into. At the same time information would be sent in that the Kellys were to be found at the head of some of the rivers, in a country quite unoccupied, and that they were living on wild cattle, away from all their friends, some 150 miles from Benalla. From time to time reliable information was obtained that they were seen in different parts, and the spies and agents employed were hearing of them.

The first active step I took, after I had been round the district and had obtained all the information I could, was to go to Beechworth to meet a well-known friend and bush telegraph of the gang, named Aaron Sherritt. He was a splendid man, tall, strong, hardy, but a most outrageous scoundrel. It was well known that he and Joe Byrne and Ned Kelly had been connected with each other in no end of horse-stealing cases, and that after the murders he had befriended the gang before they went to the Murray, as before stated. He had supplied them

AARON SHERRITT

P. 140.

with food, and guarded them against surprise. I had never seen Sherritt until that evening, and somehow or other I made a most wonderful impression upon him. I had some drink with him, and saw that my influence over him was very great. After being in his company a couple of hours, and undertaking to give him the £4000 reward that had been offered for the apprehension of the outlaws, I got him to promise he would show me where they were to be found. He told me Joe Byrne and Dan Kelly had called at his house two days before, and wanted him to accompany them to New South Wales, where they intended to rob another bank; but he was not certain which place it would be, he thought they were going to Goulburn, at least they told him so. He said he declined going with them, and they pressed him very hard, but he refused; they told him they wanted him to do the scouting for them. We doubted the truth of this statement, but at once made inquiries, and found that Joe Byrne and Dan Kelly had been seen by others going in the direction of the Murray a couple of days before, and they had called for supplies at a shanty where Byrne was well known. This information was furnished to the police on the New South Wales side of the Murray, and they were told that Goulburn was the probable place they would make for, as the Kellys had a number of relations there. About a week after this, news was telegraphed that the outlaws had stuck up the township of Jerilderie, and robbed the bank, on the 11th February 1879.

Jerilderie is a town about sixty miles from the Murray river on the New South Wales side of the border. It had a population at that time of about 300 inhabitants; there were three or four hotels, one bank, a police station with two mounted constables named Devine and Richards, and a telegraph station. The police station is situated some little distance outside the township.

About midnight on Saturday the 9th of February, Ned Kelly, Joe Byrne, Steve Hart, and Dan Kelly surrounded the police station, which was all in darkness, the constables having retired to their beds, when they were awoke by some one calling out—"Constable Devine, there is a drunken man at Davidson's hotel in the township who has committed a murder. Get up at once all of you." Constable Richards, who was up first, came outside, followed immediately afterwards by Devine, both being undressed and unarmed. Ned Kelly began to tell these men there was a great row in the township, and after conversing with them for some time, to make sure there were no other constables inside, he suddenly presented two revolvers at Devine's head, Joe Byrne doing the same to Constable Richards. The outlaws immediately procured the keys of the lock-up, took the two policemen and lodged them in their own watch-house, and locked the door. Having secured the constables, they attended to their horses, which had been left outside the station; they put them in the police stables, fed them well, and left them secure for the night. Whilst this was going on Ned Kelly went into the police station, secured all the arms belonging to the police, made the constable's wife and family go into one room, and placed Steve Hart as sentry over them, telling them if they gave the slightest alarm, that the two constables who were in the lock-up would be the first persons to be shot, and they themselves would also suffer the same death. The outlaws then made themselves as comfortable as they could, leaving one of their number on sentry until daylight on Sunday morning.

During all that day Mrs. Devine was allowed to go about the station as usual, so as not to raise any suspicion that anything unusual was going on. Ned Kelly ascertained from her, that it was her custom to clean out the church and prepare the place for service, and Joe Byrne was sent to this place of worship with Mrs. Devine, whilst she carried out her usual duties there. This took about half an hour, and they both returned to the station. No one called at the station during the day; had they done so, they would have been pounced upon and secured in the lock-up so as to prevent an alarm being given. The people attended service as usual, but no one came near the station.

Dan Kelly and Steve Hart had dressed themselves up in the police uniform, and walked about the station in a most conspicuous manner, and without attracting any attention. In the afternoon Joe Byrne dressed himself in police uniform, and with Steve Hart also in that dress, took Constable Richards out of the lock-up to accompany them round the town, in order that they might be made aware of the positions of hotels, bank, &c. They ordered the constable, in case any one came up and spoke to him, to introduce them as new constables about to be stationed there. Their walk lasted about an hour, and they again returned to the police barracks. Nothing of any note took place during the evening and Sunday night. Monday morning Joe Byrne, in uniform, took two of their

AT THE ROYAL HOTEL. 145

horses to be shod by the police farrier in the township; he waited until they were shod, and then took them back to the police station.

About eleven o'clock, after locking up the policeman's wife and children with Constable Devine, they took out Constable Richards. Ned Kelly and Dan Kelly dressed in uniform, and walked to the township, followed by Hart and Byrne on horseback. They first went to the Royal Hotel, owned by a Mr. Cox, when Constable Richards introduced Ned Kelly to Mr. Cox as Ned Kelly, who told the landlord he wanted to secure some rooms in the hotel, and that he also intended robbing the bank, but he did not want to injure any one. Ned Kelly placed the other three in certain positions, and gave each of them their instructions. Hart was placed inside the large dining-room, which was used as a room of detention, and every person who came near the hotel throughout the day was placed in this room, and all prisoners captured were taken over and kept in safety in this apartment. Byrne went to the back part of the establishment and collected all the servants, and made prisoners of them.

After this was done, they devoted their attentions to the Bank of New South Wales, in which there were three officers—Mr. Jarleton, manager,

L

Mr. Living, accountant, and Mr. Mackin, sub-accountant. Mr. Living was the only one in the bank. He heard some footsteps approaching from the back-yard, and turned round thinking it was Mr. Jarleton, when he saw a man close to him. He immediately asked this man, who had already levelled his revolver at him, who he was. His reply was "the Kelly gang," and he at once called on him to "bail up." This man afterwards turned out to be Joe Byrne. Byrne then ordered him to deliver up what fire-arms he had. Mackin, who was standing outside the bank in the street, hearing voices, went inside, and Byrne immediately ordered him to jump over the counter, at the same time pointing two revolvers at him; this order he obeyed at once. Byrne then told the two bank officials they must accompany him to Cox's hotel, remarking at the same time they had all the police stuck up. The three then went to the hotel, where they met Ned Kelly, who asked for Mr. Jarleton, and was told he was in his dressing-room. Ned Kelly and Byrne went back to the bank, but could not find him. Ned Kelly returned to Cox's and brought back Mr. Living, telling him he had better find him. Living found him in his bath, and said, "Mr. Jarleton, we are stuck up, the

ROBBING THE BANK. 147

Kellys are here, and the police are also stuck up." Byrne then brought over Dan Kelly, and left him in the bath-room in charge of the manager. Ned then took charge of Living, led him into the bank, and asked him what money they had in their keeping. Living replied, "There is between six and seven hundred pounds." Kelly replied, "You must have at least £10,000 here." Living then handed him the teller's cash, amounting to £691.

At this time a Mr. Elliot, the local school-master, entered the bank, quite unconscious of what was going on within, when Ned Kelly covered him with two revolvers and ordered him to get over the counter. Mr. Elliot replied he was unable to get over, but Kelly pretty soon made him do so. Kelly then tried to put the money into a bag, but it not being large enough to hold it, he got a bag of his own at the hotel and put the money in that. Kelly asked Living if they had any more money, and was told they had not. Kelly then went to the safe and asked what was in it, and Living said nothing of any value. Kelly insisted upon it being opened, and Living gave him one of the keys. Byrne wished to smash the safe, but Ned Kelly brought in the manager, who had been taken over to the hotel, and compelled him to give up the second key. The safe was then opened, when the sum of £1450 was taken out and placed in the bag.

Kelly then took down a large tin box from the shelf; he was told it was full of documents which were of no use. He replied, "Then I will burn them;" but Mr. Jarleton begged of him not to do so. Kelly took out one bundle of papers and put them in his pocket. He then told Mr. Jarleton he intended burning all the books in the office; however, he left the documents in the tin box, saying, "I will return directly and examine them all." They all then went to the hotel. Dan Kelly was in the bar, and Ned took him and another of the party to the back of the premises, made a fire, and burned four of the bank-books. I might mention here that Ned Kelly always posed as a friend of the working-man, and all they wanted was bank money, and not that of private individuals; and in all their exploits, if any of the gang had taken a watch, or stolen anything from a private individual, when complained of Ned had made them return it to the person from whom it was stolen. In this manner he was looked upon as a great hero, and gained a number of sympathizers, so in burning the books of the bank he thought he was protecting the poor man, as against the bank.

About this time a Mr. Rankin and a Mr. Gill, seeing

the bank door open, went in, and they were immediately followed by Ned Kelly, who ordered them to " bail up." They at once grasped the situation, Rankin running into the hotel followed by Kelly, while Gill made off in another direction. The latter was the local newspaper proprietor, the former a well-to-do merchant, and a Justice of the Peace. When Kelly got up to Rankin he asked him why he had run away when he had ordered him to stand; he caught Rankin very roughly by the collar of his coat, and ordered him into the passage away from the other prisoners, telling him to straighten himself up, as he intended to shoot him, and levelled his revolver at him. Several of the prisoners called out to Ned Kelly not to fire, and he did not do so. He then called Hart by the name of "Revenge," and ordered him to shoot the first man who showed any signs of resistance, then addressing Rankin said, "If you attempt to move, you will be the first man to be shot." Mr. Rankin was a splendid able-bodied man, but without fire-arms in his possession he was powerless, and had to submit to be thus treated. Kelly then went and directed his attention to Mr. Gill, and in company with Mr. Richards and Mr. Living went to look for him. The policeman had his revolver with him, but Kelly had previously drawn the cartridges. They sent to Gill's house, and saw his wife; Kelly said to her, "Where is your husband?" She replied, "He has run away." Kelly then said, "I have a statement here which contains a little part of my life, and I want it published by Mr. Gill, will you take it?" She declined to do so.

Mr. Living then took the paper from Kelly, promising to have it published. The bushrangers then turned their attention to the telegraph office; they removed all the clerks from the office, and took them over to the hotel and put them amongst the other prisoners. Byrne remained in the office and overhauled all the messages that had been despatched that day. Kelly then returned and found Byrne in charge; he had cut all the wires, and Ned Kelly broke the insulators with his revolver. Ned Kelly told the telegraph master, Mr. Jefferson, that if he attempted to mend the wires before next day, or offer any resistance to himself or companions, he would shoot him; he also told him that he intended to take him a few miles into the bush when he left, and then liberate him, but this he did not do. Kelly informed the company who were in the hotel, that he intended sticking up the Urana coach that night, and he would shoot any one who would warn the driver, but Mr.

Jarleton succeeded in dispatching a messenger to Urana directly the outlaws left, to warn the banks against surprise. But this was only a ruse on their part, they never stuck up the coach, nor went near Urana. When Mr. Jarleton was found in his bath he had just returned from a long ride of forty miles. He stated, when Living told him they were stuck up, he thought it was a hoax they were playing on him, but when he saw Kelly and Byrne with revolvers in each hand, he saw the mistake he had made. Mr. Jarleton made some inquiries of Hart as to the movements of the gang, but after answering one or two, he pointed his revolver at him, and in an angry tone replied, "You had better stop asking such questions."

Hart and Dan Kelly stood sentry a greater part of the day with a revolver in each hand, and the former evinced a great desire to shoot somebody in the room. Throughout the day every one who came near the hotel for any purpose was captured and detained. Occasionally one of the gang would take a walk up the street. Ned Kelly went into another hotel kept by a Mr. McDougall, entered into conversation with several people there, and said, "Any one can shoot me, but they would have to abide the consequences, as every inhabitant in the town would be shot."

Hart, who always was a thief and sneak, took a new saddle from a saddler's shop, and he also relieved several men of their watches, but when the owners complained to Ned Kelly and Byrne he was ordered to return them. Ned Kelly and his lieutenant Joe Byrne showed great judgment in the manner they carried out the whole affair. Ned Kelly took from McDougall's stable a blood mare, and promised to return it in three weeks, which of course he never did. He also took a saddle and bridle and pair of spurs belonging to Mr. Jarleton from the bank, also a pair of riding-trousers, gold watch and chain. This saddle was put on the blood mare, and Dan Kelly mounted it and rode away to try it, and returned shortly afterwards.

About six o'clock in the evening the gang began to make preparations for a start, but before doing so, Ned Kelly made a speech to those who had been confined in the hotel, with the evident intention of exciting pity. He said that on the occasion when Constable Fitzpatrick was wounded, he was not within 400 miles of his mother's place; he said he had stolen 400 horses from a squatter's run, named Mr. Whilty, at various times, and had sold them, but beyond this, up to the time he shot the police at the Wombat, he had not been guilty of any other crime. Kelly showed those present his revolvers, and pointed out one which he said was the property of Constable Lonergan, and further stated, that the musket with which he shot Lonergan was an old, worn-out, crooked thing. Kelly then took Constable Richards from amongst the prisoners and walked to the police station.

At about seven o'clock Byrne mounted his horse and started off alone in the direction of the Murray river, leading a pack-horse with the treasure strapped across the saddle. This was one of the policeman's horses, which they took with them. Shortly afterwards Ned Kelly mounted, leading another police horse, returned to Cox's hotel, and told all the prisoners they might go home, and he now released them. He left Constables Devine and Richards in the lock-up, with orders they were not to be released for some hours. Dan Kelly and Hart, before they left, rode up and down the chief street of the town flourishing their revolvers over their heads, and singing at the top of their voices, and then started in the same direction as the other bushrangers had done. They must have all met at some appointed place, for they called at a station some twenty miles distant from Jerilderie, and threatened to shoot the owner for something he had done against them.

When Mr. Gill bolted from the bank, he went to

the creek close by, and remained hidden there all day, and until the gang left the town. Both Kellys left the township wearing the police clothing. With regard to the documents Ned Kelly left with Mr. Living for Mr. Gill to publish, it was sent to the Government of Victoria, and I read it. It was a tissue of lies from beginning to end, a wandering narrative full of insinuations and complaints against the police, and of the type familiar to all who have had experience of tales which men of the criminal stamp are in the habit of telling; it is as impossible to prevent these men from lying as it is from stealing.

According to Ned Kelly, his criminal career commenced when he was fourteen years old, and received a sentence of three months' imprisonment for using a neighbour's horse without his consent, as he put it. After this, convictions were frequent, and, says Kelly, "The police became a nuisance to the family." At one period of his life Kelly described himself as a "wandering gamester." He states in this document, "When the affray with Fitzpatrick took place, the constable came to apprehend my innocent brother Dan. My mother asked him if he hàd a warrant, he replied he had a telegram. My mother said to Fitzpatrick, 'If my son Ned was here he would chuck you out of the house.' Dan looked out of the window and said, 'Here he comes.' The constable turned suddenly round to look out of the window, when Dan jumped up and seized the constable, and in the scuffle Fitzpatrick was shot through his wrist."

I quote this fully because certain newspapers in the colony published statements to the effect that Fitzpatrick had acted improperly towards Kate Kelly, and that had caused Dan Kelly to shoot Fitzpatrick, and that Ned Kelly took up his sister's cause. By this means they obtained no end of sympathy from the general public, whereas there was not one word of truth in the accusation. And Ned Kelly, not only in the statement that he gave to Mr. Living, in which he said this was a pure invention, but also after his capture, stated distinctly there was not one word of truth in the accusation made against Fitzpatrick; "for," said Ned Kelly, "if there had been, I would not have been a man had I not shot him on the spot." But from Ned Kelly's own narrative it is apparent that these charges were pure inventions, made solely for the purpose of raising sympathy for these murderers. It was admitted that Fitzpatrick was resisted and assaulted while in the execution of his duty. An account is given in this statement of Ned Kelly's of the terrible tragedy at Mansfield, but it is obviously a string of falsehoods, and it would be quite improper to have it published, but he admitted that the police were not in any way the aggressors at the Wombat, but were surprised and shot down in cold blood.

The outlaws, after the Jerilderie bank robbery, evidently returned back to their mountain retreats in Victoria. No end of Bank of New South Wales notes were in circulation shortly afterwards, but the numbers of the stolen notes were not known, beyond the fact, that the head office at Sydney had sent these identical notes to Jerilderie for circulation, but no account was kept of the notes that were paid out of the bank. Hence no prosecution could be instituted, as the bank officials could not swear the notes found in the possession of the friends of the outlaws had not been paid over the counter. Notwithstanding that all the wires of the telegraph lines were cut at Jerilderie, and the outlaws departed from there at seven o'clock, at nine o'clock that night I received a wire at Benalla from Jerilderie informing me of all the facts of the matter. I at once took steps to give instructions to all crossing-places on the Murray river to keep a sharp look out, and sent men during the night to every known crossing-place, to endeavour to effect their capture, but all to no effect. The distance between Jerilderie and Benalla, where I was stationed, was over 100 miles, and the first tidings we heard of their return was that Dan Kelly was seen two or three days after the bank robbery making back to the mountains in this colony, some fifteen miles from Beechworth.

I have written fully on the subject of this bank robbery, because the plans were well laid, and everything carried out in such an able manner. I am indebted to the newspapers of the day for refreshing my recollection of the facts that took place after the bank robbery, as I did not like to trust to my memory as to the numerous incidents that occurred during that exciting time.

The Government of New South Wales, together with the banks of that colony, offered an additional reward of £1000 for the apprehension of each of the outlaws, making the sum offered by the two colonies £8000. Sherritt told me, at my first interview with him, that he was the principal agent of the outlaws in that part of the district, and everything that was known about them by their friends would be communicated to him. Besides which he was at this time engaged to be married to Joe Byrne's sister, and she lived with her mother at Woolshed. He also told me that if they did rob a bank, they were sure to call at Mrs. Byrne's on their way back, and leave her some of the money. He said, "Now if you want really to take them, I will lay you on them." I told him I would place myself unreservedly in his hands and do whatever he suggested, and I arranged to meet him again. When he left, I told the detective who introduced him to me what he had said. The detective ridiculed the affair and said, "He is only deceiving you, sir, please don't trust him; he would not sell his friend Joe Byrne for all the money in the world." I felt convinced my opinion of the man was correct, and he meant to work for us honestly. Sherritt said "You have a most difficult and dangerous job before you, but I will do all I can to assist you." Sherritt had a most exalted opinion of Ned Kelly, and said he did not believe there was another man like him in the colony. He said, "He is about the only man I ever was afraid of in my life, and I certainly give him best in everything." When I found out that the information he had given me about the two outlaws having called at his house was correct, I felt very confident that before long we should fall across them.

CHAPTER VIII.

Aaron Sherritt—A Disappointment—At Mrs. Byrne's—A Twenty-five-day Watch—Manufacturing Brands—Sherritt's Revenge—A Letter from Joe Byrne—Whorouly Races—On Watch at Mrs. Sherritt's—Mrs. Byrne's Discovery—Break-up of the Camp—Arrest of Kelly Sympathizers—A Dynamite Scare—Aaron jilted.

DIRECTLY the bank was stuck up at Jerilderie I started off to Beechworth, and sent for Aaron Sherritt. His first words to me were, "Did I not tell you they would stick up a bank in New South Wales?" I replied, "Yes, but you told me they were going to Goulbourn." I said, "Well, what is to be done now?" He replied, "They will be back probably to-night, to Woolshed." He told me to meet him that night at a place indicated by him in the ranges (known to the detective); he would then show me where they tied up their horses, whilst they went into Mrs. Byrne's house for supper. I agreed to his suggestion, and told the detective what I had done. His reply was, "I have known

Sherritt for years, and if he likes he can put you in the position to capture the Kellys, but I doubt his doing so." I told him Aaron felt sure they would return from Jerilderie that night, and I had arranged to go with him, and meet him at eight o'clock that night at a certain spot in the ranges, which I described, a party of police accompanying us. Having no men at Beechworth, I drove the detective to Eldorado, which was beyond Woolshed, where I had a party of police stationed. As the detective was well known in the locality, and I was not, I put him in the boot of the buggy under the seat, and he remained in that position nearly all the way. I merely state this to show how cautious we had to be in all our movements. Had he been recognized driving in a buggy, the friends of the outlaws would soon have heard of it. I had to take him because he had to direct the party where to meet us that night, and I had not been in the district for very many years, and knew little of it.

At eight o'clock that night the detective and I met Aaron at the appointed spot in the ranges. We waited anxiously for the men from Eldorado to turn up. After waiting for an hour, Aaron said to me, "You will be late, Mr. Hare. We should have been nearly three miles from this by this time." I was very much annoyed at the men not keeping their appointment; and I turned to the detective and said to him: "Will you stick to me, as it will never do to lose this chance of getting the outlaws?" His reply was: "Yes, Mr. Hare, I will stick to you and do whatever you tell me to do." I turned to Aaron and said: "All right; we are ready to go with you now." He turned towards me to see if I meant it. I said, "Come on."

We mounted our horses. I followed Aaron, the detective following me. The night was terribly dark, and Aaron took us at a good pace. The country was rugged and broken, but he rode ahead just as if he was in his own garden. He appeared to trust to his horse, and I trusted to him. We rode along without a word being spoken by any of us. He might have taken me over a precipice, as I could see nothing before me. Suddenly Aaron stopped, and in a whisper said to me, "This is the bushrangers' country; no one ever comes in here but them." We were then about ten miles from Beechworth on the ranges at the back of Woolshed, and so we rode along, winding round a drain one minute, and over logs and rocks the next, trusting entirely to our horses. Suddenly Aaron pulled up, and I went up beside him, the detective doing likewise.

M

Aaron said, "They are back from Jerilderie. Do you see that fire in the distance?" I replied, "Yes." He said, "The bushrangers are there; I have never before seen a fire in this place, and for some reason they have lighted one, and there they are." We all three dismounted from our horses and sat down on the ground to decide what was to be done. Aaron said, "What do you wish me to do? I will do whatever you like." I thought "nothing venture nothing have," so I questioned him as to the fire being made by the outlaws, but he was perfectly convinced of it. I then told him the first thing I wanted to be sure of was whether the bushrangers were sitting or sleeping near the fire, and he had better take off his boots, leave his horse with me, and crawl along the ground as close to the fire as he could get, and see if he could recognize the voices if he could hear any, if not, to get as close up as he could and find out whether the outlaws were there. He never hesitated for a moment, and did exactly what I told him to do, and the detective and myself were left alone. We both were fully convinced we should have to "do or die" that night, and we were quite prepared to take the risk. We stayed in the same spot for about ten minutes, deciding how we were to make the attack, when we heard footsteps

A DISAPPOINTMENT. 163

coming towards us at a quick pace. The detective said, " He has sold us; who is this coming towards us ? " I said, " Keep quiet." We both, with revolvers in our hands, remained perfectly still until the footsteps came within a yard of us, and a voice we recognized as Aaron's said, " Mr. Hare, we have been deceived, that fire is on the opposite range and some miles away." My first thought was that Aaron had gone up to the fire and started the bushrangers off, or else had given them notice he would bring us up to them. I questioned him and he appeared perfectly honest, and said, " If you will come with me I will convince you that what I am saying is the truth."

We mounted our horses and found that what he had stated was perfectly correct. Aaron then said, " We are awfully late, we must hurry on to Mrs. Byrne's house," and we again followed him in the same order as before. He commenced to go down a fearfully steep range. I said not a word but followed him, until he pulled up and said, " I am afraid to go down here to-night, it is so very dark." I said, "Is there no other way you can get down ? " He replied, " Only by going a mile round." He said, " Be careful not to move from your saddle, for this is a terribly steep range, and if you attempt to get off you will roll down some hundreds of feet." He told me to get off the horse on the off side, he doing the same himself, and the detective also. We then led our horses round and got down another gap in the mountains. After riding about a mile Aaron told us that we had better dismount and tie our horses to a tree, and walk down to the spot he would take us to.

We did so, and we followed him down the ranges until we came to a house, which turned out to be Mrs. Byrne's, the mother of the outlaw Joe Byrne. Here also, as in Power's case, we met some watchdogs in the shape of a flock of geese, and they did give the alarm, and no mistake. However, after a short time, Aaron crawled up to the house, so as to ascertain if there was any one talking inside. Everything was quiet, there was a candle burning. He returned and said, "They expect them to-night. You see, they have left the candle burning, and some supper ready on the table." He then said, "Let us go up to a clump of trees at the back of the house, where they generally tie up their horses." I had previously been told by another agent of this clump of trees, where marks of horses having been tied up were to be seen. Aaron said to me, "Go into that clump. They often tie up their horses there, and lay down beside them and have a sleep,

UP IN THE MOUNTAINS. 165

after having their supper at Mrs. Byrne's." I walked into the clump, but found no horses there, and returned to Aaron. Aaron then said, " We must now wait in this stock-yard, which leads up to the clump. If they come they will come through here." It was then about two o'clock in the morning. We sat down and waited until daylight, and then, nothing happening, we started back to our horses, reaching Beechworth at eight o'clock.

Aaron suggested to me that I should bring a party of men and come and live in the mountains at the back of Mrs. Byrne's house. He told me he could put me in a spot which was unknown to any one except the bushrangers, and the only danger of my being discovered was by them. He said I could stay in the mountains by day, and take up my position in the stock-yard behind Mrs. Byrne's at night, and that if I had patience I was certain to get them. I complied with his suggestion, and that evening I brought a party to the spot indicated by him. We brought our blankets and some provisions, intending to stay there until we caught the Kellys, watching by night, and laying in our camp all day. In camp I arranged that no two men should be together throughout the day, whether sleeping or at meals, so that if we were attacked by the outlaws, and some of us were shot, the others could fight.

The life was extremely monotonous, for me especially; but the excitement kept us up, and we always expected that sooner or later we should come across the outlaws.

Our daily life was as follows :—At dusk in the evening, one at a time, we used to leave our camp and make down to the stock-yard, I always leading the way, and the other men following. We had to be most careful where we trod, for fear of our tracks being seen on the following day. We each took up positions behind trees outside the stock-yard, I taking the opening into the yard myself. I had given orders to the men not to move from their positions until I called to them, no matter what happened. We were all lying about ten or fifteen yards apart. The nights were bitterly cold.

Aaron used to spend his evenings at Mrs. Byrne's with his young woman, and he obtained all the information they were possessed of, and when he left their house between twelve and one o'clock he used to lie down and watch with us. He always took up his position beside me, and used to relate all kinds of encouraging reports that he had obtained during the day as to the prospect of the Kellys turning up. Hardly a night that we took up our positions but we thought we should have some luck. As day broke in the morning we used to make back to our camp in the mountains in a very disappointed mood, walking singly, and avoiding the paths or soft places, so as not to leave any tracks behind us.

The great danger I felt was a surprise when getting into the camp of a morning and taking up our positions in the evening. I felt sure that some morning or evening when we took up our post the Kellys would find out our camps and take possession of them, so therefore I always went into camp first in the morning and left it first in the evening, and felt a relief when we all got into our places without being fired on. We dared not make a fire for fear of the smoke being noticed, so we had to live on water, preserved beef, and bread. I stayed in this camp for twenty-five days, and during that time, although we used to see some members of the Byrne family passing to and fro, they never discovered our whereabouts. I always kept a sentry by day over the camp, and the sentry's position was behind a rock near the spot I had made my resting-place, which was the highest, above all the men.

Night after night Aaron used to go and see his young woman, and bring back hopes of success.

This used to keep up the spirits of the men, and we all felt sure if we could keep watching without our whereabouts being discovered we would eventually be successful.

I should have stated before this, that when I went with my party into the mountains, I also placed four men in a spot pointed out to me by Sherritt, which was one of the camps used by the Kellys. It was here they stayed for two days after the murders, while Aaron supplied them with food. It was a wonderfully romantic spot, on the edge of a precipice, and only approachable on one side. Two men could keep off a dozen. This camp was placed under Senior Constable Mayes, a bold, trustworthy, well-tried man, in whom I had the utmost confidence. He had a difficulty in getting water for his men, and had to send two miles for it. Sometimes the men were sent by day, but generally by night, and through an indiscretion on the part of one of these men, our whereabouts was discovered. Old Mrs. Byrne was a most active old party. She was constantly looking about for the tracks of police, horses, and men. She was walking along the bank of a creek where the men at the upper camp were in the habit of getting their water, when she discovered a spot where a man had been sitting and amusing himself with a stick — as it is called, "whittling" it. She immediately came to the conclusion that some police were camped close by, and that night she confided her fears to Aaron, and told him he must have a good look in the ranges next day. He promised to make every effort to find out if her surmise was correct, and he came straight to the stock-yard where I was watching, and informed me of the discovery the old woman had made. Aaron next day got his horse and pretended to make a search, returning next night and telling Mrs. Byrne he could find no trace of anybody. The old lady was convinced there must have been some police about, because she said the footmarks were evidently those of a policeman. These people appear to know the difference between the footprints of police and other persons. However, the old woman could not be convinced she was wrong, and up to that time had perfect faith in Aaron, and so also had his young woman, her daughter.

Generally when we left the stock-yard in the morning, Sherritt would leave us and go to his own hut on the ranges, or else to his father's place, which was between our camp and Beechworth; but sometimes he would come into our camp and get his breakfast, and perhaps stop a part of the day. Very often he had to carry provisions for us from Beechworth during the night. He was always ready to do anything for me, and yet many of the men distrusted him. I never did from the first moment I took up with him, and his end showed I was right in my opinion of him. Of a night, whilst I was watching with him, he would sit beside me and tell me the adventures of his life, and give me information of many things that were formerly unexplained. He told me how he, Joe Byrne, and Ned Kelly used to steal horses wholesale, and how they used to dispose of them, and the way they changed the brands of the horses so that the most experienced hand would not discover the trick. It was as follows:—Supposing a horse was branded H on the near shoulder, they would turn the H into H B (conjoined) by getting a pair of tweezers, pulling out the hairs to make a B, and then prick the skin with a needle dipped in iodine. This burns up the skin, and for about a month afterwards it looks like an old brand; new brands were also put on in this fashion, and they never could be detected. After branding the horses they had collected, they would make for some squatter's station where they were unknown, ask permission to put their horses into his stock-yard, on the pretence that they had met a stranger who wanted to purchase the mob of horses, this stranger being one of their own party. Generally speaking, the squatter or some one belonging to the station would walk down to look at the horses, and he would hear them making bargains about the price of each animal, so as to lead the people of the station to believe that it was a genuine sale. At last they would agree to a price, and then would ask the squatter to allow them to go into his office to draw up a receipt, in which all the brands would be entered, both old and manufactured ones. After the receipt had been drawn up the squatter would be asked to witness it, and the supposed buyers would start off towards Melbourne, and the seller appear to return back to New South Wales. If by chance any of the horses were claimed by their owners, the receipt would be produced, and they would so avoid being arrested.

Aaron used to tell me they made raids on horses from about Wagga to Albury, took them a back track to Melbourne, and on their return would pick up a number of horses in Victoria and take them over to Wagga or Albury for sale. One of the party used to act as the master, and the others as his servants; the master always going ahead and making arrangements where the horses were to be paddocked for the night.

For hours did Aaron relate anecdotes to me of the same description as the above, and he enlightened me greatly into the ways and the life of horse-stealers. I cannot refrain from telling another of his stories. I was sitting beside him one night, when he had brought us some very hopeful information, and we were all very elated at our prospect of success. I said, "Well, Aaron, I feel sure you will get the reward offered for the Kellys." (I had promised him he should have the whole sum of £8000 if it was upon his information that the Kellys were captured.) At this time his young woman was getting rather suspicious that he was working for the police, although she used to meet him of an evening very near our camp and walk with him. I asked him how he would like the reward disposed of, supposing he got it? He said, "I should like to have a few mares and an entire horse, and get a nice farm." I told him he should get a respectable girl, marry her, leave all his old associates, and begin life again amongst new people. He agreed with all I said, and turned round and said to me, "Mr. Hare, do you think, if you got me the best mares you could buy, and got me the best entire horse you could purchase, that I could withstand the temptation of taking my neighbour's horses and selling them? No, I could not, no more than fly."

On another occasion we were expecting the outlaws to bring some money they had stolen from the bank to Mrs. Byrne's. Amongst my men I had one who was a thorough larrakin, and Aaron took a great fancy to him. I sent him to Beechworth for some supplies, and Aaron met him on the way, and they both rode into Beechworth together. My man was taken for one of the Kelly spies, especially as he was in Aaron's company. The people of Beechworth at once became alarmed, seeing Aaron and his companion riding about the streets—no one knowing the companion was a policeman. Numbers of people went at once to the police station and reported that Aaron and another suspicious person, riding good horses, were seen in the outskirts of the town. The constable was delighted to have a chance of being seen with Aaron, and made the most of his opportunity.

On the way back to my camp Aaron took the constable into his confidence; he told him that he felt certain that the bushrangers would return from Jerilderie after they had stuck up the bank there, and the first place they would come to was Mrs. Byrne's. Aaron said to him, "I want you to join me in a scheme, and if it comes off we shall have the best of the arrangement." The constable said, "What is it?" He replied, "I feel sure the Kelly gang will return from Jerilderie either to-night or during the course of this week. Joe Byrne will be leading a packhorse, with the gold and notes fastened up in a brown cloth coat. Directly Mr. Hare opens fire on the men, the pack-horse will, in all probability, break away with the treasure. You and I can go after the horse, catch him, and take his pack off in the bush, hide it, and let the horse go; and next day, in the excitement, we can slip away and divide the cash. It can do no harm to any one, because some one will get it, and we might just as well have it as anybody else." The constable appeared to agree to Aaron's suggestion, and told me what had passed between them. I told him not to tell any one else in camp about the arrangement, and to lead Aaron to believe that he would assist him in the matter. Unfortunately the Kellys did not put in an appearance, and so the matter fell through.

I must give one more narrative about Aaron, just to show the peculiar kind of man he was, even on the chance of being thought tedious. He came to me one morning and said, " Mr. Hare, I want to go away for a couple of days to look after some cattle of mine. I will be back within two days." I questioned him closely, what cattle he was going after, and asked him if he wanted any money. I had not engaged him at any fixed salary, but whilst he was watching with me he used to ask me for a pound or two, and I gave it to him. He often refused to take money from me, as he thought I was paying him out of my own pocket, whereas the Government refunded me all I paid him, and he only took sufficient to pay his expenses. Before he started off after his cattle, I said to him, " Are you sure you have got enough money to pay your way?" He replied, " I have a pound of the money you gave me last time;" and away he started, and returned according to his promise.

Some few days after this, Mrs. Byrne went to the police station, and reported that a valuable horse of hers had been stolen from Woolshed, and, after inquiry by the police, it was found in the possession of Mrs. Skillian, Ned Kelly's sister. She produced a receipt for it, as having purchased it from Aaron, and signed by him, for the small sum of £3 or £4. Mrs. Byrne obtained a warrant for Aaron's arrest, for they all suspected he was then a spy of mine. I spoke to Aaron on the subject, and he admitted that he had taken the horse and sold it to Mrs. Skillian. He said, "I could not help doing this. I did not want the horse, but I felt I must do something to old Mrs. Byrne. She has not behaved well to me lately, and her conduct towards me is so cool that I could not resist the temptation of stealing her horse."

All the time Aaron was with me, only the police who were actually in my party were aware he was working for me, and most of the others were delighted to hear there was a warrant out for his arrest. They made every effort to capture him, but could not find him. I was greatly annoyed with him, because it crippled his usefulness immensely. However, he kept out of the way of the police, and when I was relieved from the district I left it to my successor to get him out of his difficulty. I don't quite know how this was managed, but I was told he was directed to be at a certain spot one day, and a constable was ordered to go there and apprehend him. The constable afterwards took great credit for his capture, not knowing that his arrest was an arranged matter. He was brought before the police-court, but the evidence was not sufficient for the magistrates to commit him for trial, as the horse was not forthcoming, and Aaron was acquitted. I am not quite sure I am right in all the details of what occurred with reference to his arrest, but I was told that this was how the matter was managed.

A number of letters fell into our hands written by the outlaws, most of them by Joe Byrne. He was, for a bushman, rather clever with his pen, but I do not intend to disclose how we became possessed of them. However, I got one addressed to Aaron Sherritt, Sheepwash Creek, near Beechworth. This was the address of his father. I opened it and could not understand a word of it, as it was written in bush slang. I at once went for my boy Tommy, as I christened him, for Aaron was too uncommon a name to be constantly using. In sending telegrams concerning him to the members of the force who knew him, I always called him Tommy, for had I used his name, every one would have guessed who Aaron was. As I said, I sent for Tommy, and met him on a large granite rock at the back of Beechworth. I showed the letter to him. He looked at me and said,

"How did you get this into your possession?" I said, "Never mind, read it to me; and who is it from?" He said, "Why, from Joe Byrne, of course." He sat down and read the letter without the least difficulty. I could not make head nor tail of it. I had the original, but I don't know what became of it. The purport of the letter was to the following effect. The writer told Aaron to be at the Whorouly races, which were to take place within a week, and where to meet him, at the back of the course, ordering him not to say a word about their going to the course. He also said that he had the black mare which Aaron had ridden in a steeplechase previously, and that the mare was in good order and sure to win. I asked Aaron what he thought best to be done? He said, "You must give me a good horse to ride to the races, and I will assist in every way possible."

I consulted with my brother officer as to what was best to be done, and we decided to send the usual mounted constables in uniform, and we then selected three good riders amongst the men, who were unknown in the district, and sent them separately to the races. They were all splendid riders and magnificently mounted. The men and horses could have been backed against the Kelly gang, man for man, at anything. We also arranged that I should ride out myself and appear to take great interest in the races. I did go out, and saw the three constables in plain clothes. One had a table and was playing the three-card trick; another had erected an Aunt Sally, and was bawling out at the top of his voice, and the third kept on his horse riding about. I was more afraid of the third man than any of the others, because he was a most excitable fellow and bold, and as good a rider as ever sat on a horse, but with no discretion. He would have faced the four outlaws if he had had the chance, and shot them one after another if it were possible. I may as well give the names of these men. They were the most dashing of all my party. The first was Tommy Lawless; the second, Faulkner; the third, Johnstone; three pluckier fellows never trod the earth. My fear was that the mounted police on duty would arrest some of my men for gambling, as they were not known to each other; but they were not interfered with.

After Lawless had been playing his three-card trick for some time, he thought he would enter his horse for the steeplechase that Aaron was supposed to ride in, thinking he would thus have a better opportunity of seeing everything all round the course. At the time appointed for this race to come off, we were all looking very anxiously for Aaron to turn up on the black mare, but alas, we were disappointed. I saw him anxiously looking out in the direction he thought the mare would appear from, but there were no signs of it. Joe Byrne's brother (Paddy) was a good deal with Aaron all that day, but the subject of Joe was not mentioned by either of them to each other. Lawless rode in the steeplechase and won it, and that was the only bit of excitement during the day.

An incident occurred during the steeplechase that I must state, although it is against the discipline of my men. Just before the steeplechase started, Johnstone saw three men riding outside the course; he took it for granted they were the outlaws. Without a moment's consideration, he galloped off alone towards them. I saw him do this, as I was wondering who the men were, and at a glance saw they could not be the Kellys. Faulkner was at the time on his horse close beside me, in the middle of a crush. He looked at me. I shook my head, and he remained where he was. I walked quietly out of the crowd, and Faulkner followed me, and we saw Johnstone returning terribly ashamed of himself. He could give me no explanation of his conduct beyond saying he could not help himself. He thought the three men were the outlaws, and he made straight for them.

Aaron Sherritt was noticed by every one riding a magnificent horse which I had purchased a few days before. He was pointed out to me by several people as Kelly and Byrne's greatest friend. I was asked why I did not have him arrested for stealing the horse he was riding, as he never could afford to come honestly by such an animal. I pleaded ignorance about either man or horse.

At night a ball was to take place at a public-house near the racecourse. We thought probably some of the gang might put in an appearance there; but there was no sign of them again, and we had to return disappointed.

In writing this narrative I have not kept exactly to the order in which the things occurred. As I have no paper to refer to, I am simply trusting to memory. After a time all the men, both in my camp and the upper, came to believe most thoroughly in Aaron's honesty of purpose, as I had done from the beginning. He often told me that I had a kind of influence over him that no other man had ever had before, and he could not tell me a lie. We kept watching as from the first. Old Mrs. Byrne began to be very doubtful of Aaron, and treated him very coolly; still the daughter believed in him, and he continued his visits to the house. The old woman was constantly abusing him, and telling him that she thought he had thrown his old friend overboard and was working for the police. Yet, notwithstanding this, the whole of Kelly's friends used to confide in him, and tell him all the movements of the police in the district, which he would repeat to me.

One night he returned, as was his custom, to where I was watching. He appeared rather anxious, and said, "Is there any news of the Kellys?" I said, "No; why do you ask?" He replied, "What is the meaning of all the activity that has taken place among the police to-day in different parts of the district?" I said, "What do you mean?" He replied, "This morning at four o'clock two men left Beechworth, and went in the direction of Woolshed. Three other men started early in the morning from Eldorado, going in the direction of Woolshed, and some three or four men started in the direction of Wangaratta." I was perfectly amazed at the organization of the sympathizers thus to have ascertained the movements of the police. I said, "Tommy, tell me how you get all this information." He replied, "I could not do that, but you would be perfectly astounded if you knew how much we know of the movements of the police."

To test whether his information was correct, I inquired, and found every word he said was true; but I never was able to find out how he obtained his information. I asked him if all the agents in the district knew as much as he did. His reply was, "Oh, yes, but I am the head over all of them."

I was in the habit, whilst with my cave party, of getting all information of everything that was going on throughout the district concerning the Kellys. One evening Detective Ward came to my camp and told me that Dan Kelly had been seen near Myrtleford, riding in the direction of Beechworth. Half an hour afterwards Aaron, on his way to Mrs. Byrne's, called in at my camp. I told him that Dan Kelly had been seen that day.

He started up at once, and said, "Then he will call at my mother's place to-night, or else at my hut, which is about two miles from my mother's;" and added, "I wish, Mr. Hare, you would bring a couple of men with you, and come with me to my mother's place; some of the gang are sure to call there if they are passing by. Let the remainder of the party go to the usual place at the stock-yard and watch Mrs. Byrne's. You come with a couple of men to my mother's place, and get two men from the upper camp and put them in my house."

I consented to this suggestion, and he accompanied me. I left two men at his house, one of whom knew the outlaws, and I went with two men to his mother's. I had a conversation with his mother, and she asked me to be careful and not to shoot any of her sons. She had two besides Aaron, Jack and Willie. I went inside their barn—a large open building, within a few yards of their dwelling-house. It was filled with straw, and the two nights I spent in that building with my two men beggars description. The pigs slept in the straw, and the fleas beat anything I ever felt in all my life; the mice, also, were running over me, and I really believe that a snake went over me also; but there was a chance of the Kellys coming there, and that was enough for us. I had arranged with Mrs. Sherritt that if she heard footsteps, or any one coming to the place during the night, she would call out, as a signal, " Is that you, Jack, or Willie ? " and I could hear their reply. Aaron stayed all night in his mother's house, in case the outlaws called to see him.

Once or twice during the night I heard footsteps approaching the house, and, of course, my heart was in my mouth, expecting it might be the welcome visitors; but, alas! Mrs. Sherritt came to the door when the dogs barked, and called out, "Is that you, Jack?" and the answer was, "Yes." I stayed there a second night, but at daylight next morning I got up and left with my two men. The horrors of that place frequently come before me, and I shudder when I think of the hours I spent in that barn.

On my way to my camp I called at Aaron's hut, picked up the two men I had left there two nights previously, and took up my position under the rock, feeling as if I had got home again; the bare rock was paradise compared with the abominable place I had just left.

I must now come to the closing act of my stay at the camp in the mountains. We had been about twenty-three nights watching there. Our breakfast consisted of bread and sardines, and a drink of water; dinner and supper the same, varied with tinned beef. In the midst of our camp was a large stone, which was used as a table. We never could have a fire. The food, whatever there was, was placed on the stone. Each man would get up from his position, take what he wanted, and go back to where his rifle lay, and eat the food there; no two men went to the so-called table at the same time.

On the last morning of my stay there, Aaron, who had been watching with us all the night, came into the camp with us. It was a Sunday morning. After we had our meal, each of us lay down in the spots we had selected and fell asleep. I was the highest up the hill, and could look down upon all the others; near me sat the sentry, and Aaron had lain down the furthest down the hill, in a hollow below a large rock. At about eight o'clock in the morning the sentry, without moving from his post, called me, and said the old woman, meaning Mrs. Byrne, was in the camp. I sat up in my cave and looked out, and saw her stealing up. She stood for a moment, saw articles lying about the camp, then came a few steps further on, looked down in the direction of where one of the men was lying, then halted for a moment, and retreated. The camp was so situated that unless a person got within a yard or two of it, he could not be seen. I watched her, and did not even let her know that we had seen her. Directly she left I jumped up and went to see who it was she had seen, and to my horror I found it to be poor Aaron. I called him up. He was lying partly on his side, and I was not certain she could have recognized who it was. I told Aaron what had happened, and he turned deadly pale, and huge drops of perspiration broke out on his face. He could scarcely speak, and gasped, "Now I am a dead man." I told him the best thing he could do now was to be off as hard as he could, and go and show himself to some of his friends, so that if Mrs. Byrne had recognized him he could prove an *alibi*, and convince her she was mistaken.

Aaron always wore a peculiar dress, and would have been known by any one at any distance. His dress consisted of a white shirt, a pair of trousers and long boots, with his trousers tucked inside. The first thing I did before I let him leave the camp was to send a sentry over the hill to see if anything could be seen of the old woman. He returned in a few minutes and pointed her out on a hill opposite to us.

I should here describe the formation of the country we were hidden in, to make myself understood. We were on the one side of a deep gully, with high hills, quite impassable to horsemen, in front and behind us. A road or track ran at the foot of the gully, and on one side of the track, about 100 yards from the bottom of this gully, was our watching-place, about half a mile from Mrs. Byrne's house. We remained quite quiet, and watched her go up the opposite hill to something white that was on a rock. This was her shawl, which she had left behind. It afterwards turned out that she was searching for the police in the mountains, and when she got to the spot where we saw her pick up her shawl, she had noticed a sardine-tin on the rock in our camp shining in the sun. This had been inadvertently left there after breakfast. When she saw this shining thing, she left her shawl and went to see what it was, and after being in our camp she returned and picked up her shawl (this she afterwards told Aaron). I put a watch over her, and saw her come down the hill again.

When she was out of sight I put my hat and great-coat on Aaron, and started him off over the back of our camp, so that if the old woman had seen him walking away she could not have recognized him. When he was gone, we set ourselves to watch the old woman closely, as she was bent on finding out how many men we had there. She was evidently under the impression that she had not been seen by any one in the camp. She descended the hill and commenced ascending the one behind us. We could see her crawling down the hill upon her hands and knees, evidently with the object of looking into our camp to see what she could. I told Senior-constable Mills to go up the hill and give her a good fright and drive her off. He ascended the hill in the direction he saw her coming down, unobserved by her, and lay behind a rock with his rifle in his hand. The old woman came down to the very rock he had taken shelter behind, and just as she was going to take a good observation of our camp, the senior-constable sprang upon her and roared out. She almost died of fright. She had not the slightest idea any one was near her. For a moment she shook from head to foot, but soon recovered herself and began to slang the senior-constable, and tell him she would get her son with the Kellys to shoot the lot of us, as they did Kennedy's party. After some conversation she left and went back to her home.

Nothing transpired that day until dusk, when Aaron reappeared as usual. I asked him what he had done with himself after leaving me that morning. He said he had gone to an intimate friend of his and shown himself, and some time afterwards had drawn attention to the early hour at which he had called. I asked him what he intended doing, if he meant to go that evening to see his young woman. He said, "Oh, yes, I must go and see if the old woman recognized me this morning." I said, "Don't you funk it?" He replied artfully, "But I must find out if she knows it was me." He went on, "I have brought a penny whistle, and I will commence playing it within a hundred yards of the house, and perhaps my girl may come out to meet me, and I can find out from her whether the old woman has said anything about me."

He left us just as we were going to the watching-place, and about twelve o'clock came as usual and sat down beside me. He told me he went with his whistle straight to the door of the house, but his young woman did not come out to meet him. He walked inside and continued playing. When he got inside, there was a strange man (a neighbour) in the room. The old woman said nothing to him, but he said, "I watched her countenance, and I felt sure she had not recognized me." After a little while, the old woman went outside, and he followed her. She said, "A nice trick you have been playing on me." He said, "What do you mean?" She said, "Who could have put the police into that camp in the mountains but you?" He replied, "I don't know what you mean." She told him how she had discovered our camp, and said there were thirty men in it. He pleaded ignorance, but she said she felt certain he knew all about it. She asked him how it was that she could find us out and he could not.

He replied he could not tell. She said, "Well, you go there to-morrow and see for yourself."

From that time I thought it was useless my remaining there any longer, but all my men begged me to stay, and so did Aaron. I stayed for two nights longer, but two old women discovered our watching-place. My men and Aaron pleaded that Mrs. Byrne had no means of communicating with the outlaws, as she did not know where they were to be found, and they were sure to seek Aaron out before going to her place. However, I could not see the use of staying any longer, so I left, though the men remained for two or three weeks longer. I was not sorry to leave the spot. It was a most uncomfortable place to sleep in. The days were terribly hot and the nights bitterly cold.

One circumstance occurred whilst watching which I think worthy of relating. About ten o'clock at night we were all in our positions, I at the opening of the stock-yard, lying under a post-and-rail fence with an old log fence at the bottom, as close to it as I could get, the men lying behind trees. There were six of us in all. I heard the footsteps of a man coming down the track from the hills. The footsteps came closer and closer, until I saw the figure of a man step on to the rails just above me. At the moment I thought it was most likely to be Joe Byrne coming down to see his mother, and I was just in the act of springing up as he jumped down, when I remembered that Aaron was down at the house, and if it was one of the outlaws he would be able to give us notice. So I decided to let him pass me. He walked right through the midst of my men. Not one of them moved, because I had not moved. He went straight to the house. About two hours afterwards Aaron came to us. I waited to see if he would say if there was any one there or not. He did not. I asked him if there were any strangers at Mrs. Byrne's. He said, " Yes, a man named Scotty, who lives up on the hills, came there." Somehow or other I fancy the man was Joe Byrne. I have no real reason for thinking so, but I do, and we let him slip past us. Aaron vowed it was not, but at the time Aaron was very partial towards his old school-fellow, Joe Byrne, and frequently he used to ask me to give Joe a chance of his life if they came into the stock-yard, but he used to say, " Of course if he fights and shoots at you, you must do the same to him."

About this time it was deemed desirable to arrest a number of the sympathizers who were setting the police at open defiance. They were galloping round the search parties, watching the movements of the

JOE BYRNE.

ARREST OF THE KELLY SYMPATHIZERS. 193

police and insulting the men. With the sanction of the Government, we decided to get together all the members of the force in charge of stations and allow them to submit the names of persons whom they knew to be Kelly sympathizers, aiding the gang by giving them information of our movements, and in other ways. The arrest was ordered of about twenty relatives and friends, and the arrests were made all over the district on the same day. They were charged with aiding and abetting the Kelly gang, and were brought before the court and remanded for a week. No evidence was given beyond the fact that they were known to be Kelly sympathizers, but upon this statement the magistrates remanded them from time to time for seven days. They were in confinement for some two or three months, but still the Kellys were able to find ways and means of supporting themselves and keeping out of the clutches of the police. At last the police magistrate, Mr. Foster, refused to remand them any longer, and discharged the whole of them. It was my painful duty, week after week, to go up to Beechworth every Friday and apply for a further remand for seven days, without being able to adduce a tittle of evidence against them. This move was a very unfortunate one. It did no good, and evoked sympathy for the men in custody. The police, I found out, had no evidence against these persons beyond the fact that they were known to be associates, relatives, and friends of the outlaws. Had the women been arrested, such as Kelly's sisters, the act might have done some good, but it was thought advisable not to interfere with the women. During the time I and several of the police were going up every Friday night to Beechworth to apply for the remand of the prisoners next morning, I had to take the constables who knew these sympathizers every week to Beechworth with me, for I never knew when the magistrates might call for some evidence, in default of which they might discharge the prisoners. As these men had been arrested we were determined to keep them as long as we could, in the hopes that the outlaws might get infuriated at all their friends being locked up on their account, but they took not the slightest notice of it.

A few weeks before those arrested were discharged, some of our spies, or, as we used to call them, "agents," gave me information that the Kellys had procured some dynamite and intended blowing up the train out of revenge for our locking up these persons. I took no notice of the report. On one Monday night the telegraph operator at Benalla informed me that for some reason the wires would not act between Beechworth and Benalla. The break was somewhere between Wangaratta and Beechworth, and the stoppage occurred about nine o'clock. The following morning the lines were found to be working all right again. The same thing occurred on Tuesday, and on Wednesday night telegraph repairers from Melbourne were sent along the line, but could find nothing wrong. Still, each evening, exactly at nine o'clock, no messages could be sent, and sometimes the line stopped working in the middle of a message. Thursday night the same thing occurred, and yet the line was not broken. One of the operators told me he believed the break was due to some one putting a piece of wire over the telegraph line and so making a ground connection. However, the cause was not discovered.

Friday night came, and we were just starting for Beechworth by the passenger train at about eight o'clock, when the operator at Benalla sent a message to me at the platform, telling me that the wire had stopped at about seven-thirty o'clock that night. I remembered then the information I had received about the line being blown up with dynamite. The officer in charge of the district and myself held a short consultation as to whether we should stop the train and inform the passengers of the danger impending. We, however, decided to get into the train and say nothing until we got to Wangaratta, when we could decide on the best course to adopt. We got into a carriage with two Roman Catholic priests who were chaffing us all the way up about not catching the Kellys. Still we said nothing about the information we received. At Wangaratta we decided to go on to Tarrawingee, as it was between that station and Beechworth the break in the line was known to be. When I got to Tarrawingee I went to the station-master and told him to stop the train until I gave him permission to start. He said he had no authority to stop the train. I then took a constable to the engine-driver and told the driver he was on no account to start without my permission, telling him at the same time of my suspicions. The officer in charge of the district and myself then called the telegraph operator whom we had in the carriage, and asked him if he could tell in any way whether the line was open between that station and Beechworth, as there was no telegraph office at Tarrawingee. The operator said if he could get up the pole and take the wire between his teeth he could tell. The difficulty was to get him up the pole, but we got a long spar and shoved him up, and he discovered connection was open again to Beechworth. The officer in charge of the district and myself then decided that we would let the train go on and say nothing at all to the passengers, who, during the detention at Tarrawingee, were calling out and grumbling at our keeping the train all that time. We got into the train and arrived safely at Beechworth, without the passengers knowing anything about the danger they had been in.

The feeling of alarm over the Kelly gang was so strong at this time, that had we raised an alarm the passenger traffic on the line would have been entirely stopped. I have often thought what a terrible thing it would have been if that train had been blown up, especially going over some of the steep embankments on the line to Beechworth. For months afterwards the Government placed men on watch to prevent the line being interfered with by the Kellys. I remember distinctly saying to my brother officers, " Well, whatever happens, we shall be in the thick of it, so they cannot blame us." I also remember the feeling of relief we both experienced when the train arrived safely at Beechworth. It was a terrible responsibility on our shoulders, and we had very little time to decide the best course to adopt, but fortunately the course we adopted turned out all right. A few days after this occurrence I was told by one of our "agents" that arrangements had been made that night to blow up the train with dynamite, but the outlaws did not know how to use the cartridges that they had been supplied with, and they were afraid to make the attempt and fail, and so resolved to defer the dynamite business to some future occasion.

After leaving the cave party, as it was called, I went to Benalla and organized several search parties, took charge of one of them myself, and had no end of adventures. My principal place of searching was the Warby Ranges, and many a hard day have I spent in them. We were trying to keep a constant watch over the relatives of the outlaws, more especially over Kelly's sister, whose place was near Greta, within four or five miles of Glenrowan. The Warby Ranges run just to the back of Glenrowan. The constables used to watch the house to see if any one arrived or left during the night. Mrs. Skillian and Katie were aware they were being watched, and nearly every night before they went to bed they would take their dogs and hunt round the bush within several hundred yards of their house. Very often the dogs discovered the police lying on the ground, and then commenced barking at them until the women came up. It appeared as if the dogs knew the police were their natural enemies. At first I used to make one of my men in the search party carry a lot of poisoned baits, and every now and then drop a bait in a likely place, but afterwards all the dogs went about day and night with muzzles on, which were only taken off when they were being fed.

This puts me in mind of another incident in our search. Information came that the Kellys were expected on the following day, Sunday, to visit a cousin of theirs, Tom Lloyd, a man who was a notorious sympathizer, and who made no secret of it. Katie Kelly had been seen riding from her place to her cousin's with a large bundle in front of her saddle, which was supposed to be clean clothes, &c. for her brothers. I was not at Benalla when the news came in, but Aaron Sherritt happened to be there waiting for me, and Captain Standish sent out three men with Aaron to watch the place. They left Benalla in a wagon, and were driven out to within three miles of the spot where they intended watching. Lloyd lived in a house at the foot of a very high hill, in fact the mountains surrounded the house on three sides. Aaron and the three men kept off the road, and did not go within 300 yards of Lloyd's house. They took up their position in a thick clump of trees, and got there before daylight in the morning. They had a good view of Lloyd's house and the surrounding country. Shortly after daylight they saw a boy come out of the house and unfasten the dogs. They at first thought he was going to fetch the cows in to milk, but in a very short time they discovered that the boy had been sent out with the dogs to see if any one had been about the place during the night. To their horror they saw the dogs coming on their trail straight towards them, and they actually followed their footsteps into the clump of trees. One of the men jumped up, as they did not wish Aaron to be seen, and immediately the dogs began to bark. The boy ran back to the hut, and shortly afterwards the inmates came out and looked in the direction where the men had been hiding. Several shots were fired from the house, presumably as a signal, and Lloyd got an axe and struck a log of wood, which was so placed that when it was hit the sound was heard all round the hills. This also was supposed to be a signal of alarm in case the outlaws were anywhere in the neighbourhood. The men had to remain where they were all day, as it would never have done to have allowed Aaron to be seen with the police.

Shortly after the cave party was broken up, Miss Byrne broke off her engagement with Aaron, and he was free to look out for some other girl. He suggested to me that he might try Katie Kelly, and see if she would engage herself to him. He went there, but Mrs. Skillian objected to his being about the place. Katie and he got on very well, but she never mentioned her brother's name to him, nor he to her. They became very great friends. One night, when Mrs. Skillian went to see a friend, she left Katie and Aaron in the house together. Aaron induced Katie to come out for a walk with him, and when Mrs. Skillian returned she found them both away. She was most indignant, and went to the nearest police station, Oxley, and laid some charge against Aaron. The police constable went to the Kellys' house, and when Aaron saw him coming up to the door he bolted out the back way. The constable followed him, and fired a couple of shots, but could not overtake him. I received a report next day from the constable, who stated that to stop Aaron he had fired a shot at him. Aaron made his way to a schoolmaster's house that night, a place where the Kelly gang used to frequent. He borrowed a horse and rode into Beechworth, where he went straight to Detective Ward and reported the circumstance to him, asking the detective to wire to me to come up to see him at Beechworth, as he was afraid of being arrested by the police. This occurrence, strange to relate, never got into the press, and the constable at Oxley was very much surprised at the leniency shown towards Aaron. On one occasion Aaron came down to Benalla to see me. He was unobserved, arriving by train. I met him in the bush, on the banks of the Broken river. At dusk he went to the railway platform to await the train to Beechworth. When he was seen there, there was great excitement, as he was known to be Aaron Sherritt, the principal agent of the Kelly gang. A messenger was immediately sent to me in breathless haste to come quickly to the railway station. I pretended to be very much surprised, but, of course, Aaron did not recognize me nor I him, and I saw him leave by the train.

CHAPTER IX.

Mrs. Skillian's Hoax—A False Alarm—Searching the Warby Ranges—Among the Kelly Sympathizers—Ill and dispirited—The Tenant of the Haystack—Relieved after Eight Months' Camping Duty.

IT was perfectly wonderful how all the trains were watched by Kelly sympathizers. You could tell them in a moment, they were to be seen on every railway station. It is not to be understood that all these men could communicate with the outlaws; my opinion is they trusted no one but their own blood relations, but the information concerning the police was sent to persons like Aaron Sherritt, there being perhaps three or four men in the whole district who could communicate to the outlaws' sisters any information that was obtained concerning the movements of the police. Hart had a brother and sister, and they were always on the move. Byrne had a brother and two or three sisters; the former was always riding about.

Reports came in that Mrs. Skillian used to be seen at all hours of the night riding about the bush, sometimes with large packs on her saddle.

A curious incident occurred one morning about daylight. Some policemen had got to Mrs. Skillian's house about two o'clock in the morning, and were within a short distance of her place, and in some way she must have become aware of their presence there. She went into the paddock about three or four o'clock, caught her horse, saddled it and tied a large bundle on the saddle, mounted the horse, and started off towards the mountains, the three policemen following her, but without the slightest idea that she was aware of their presence. She made for a very steep gap in the mountains, the men following on foot, thinking they had a good thing on hand. The sun was nearly up when they reached the top of the gap, and the first thing they saw was Mrs. Skillian sitting on a log facing them, and her two hands extended from her nose, and taking what is called a "lunar" at them, with a grin of satisfaction on her face. They went up to examine the pack on the saddle, and found it to be an old table-cloth wrapped up evidently to take a rise out of the police, who had been watching her.

After I left the cave party, I was constantly on the move. My object was to harass the outlaws as much as possible. I had parties of men out in every direction, going all day, and watching for fires at night. I remember on one occasion I had been out in the bush for about ten days with a party, and having consumed our provisions, we came back to Benalla. The evening I returned Captain Standish got a letter evidently from a well-to-do farmer, who stated that he had on the previous evening seen four men walking in the direction of a certain man's house, giving a description of the place, and how to find it out. He gave his reasons for thinking they were the Kellys, and altogether it appeared a very good opportunity of falling across them. Captain Standish was in great glee about the information, and I remember sitting up half the night with him talking about it.

At twelve o'clock I went round to my men, awoke them, and told them to be ready to start with me at four o'clock next morning. We were up again about three, got our horses and provisions ready, and away we started at daylight, and went through the town of Benalla before any one was up. As it was Sunday morning, and it was an unusual thing for us to start away on that day, instead of going in the direction indicated in the letter, I went directly in the opposite one. When I got into the bush, about five miles from Benalla, I dismounted the men and read the letter to them. I was afraid to do so before, in case the information we were going on might leak out. They were all in great spirits at the probabilities of success, and thought our chances very good. We camped and let our horses feed in the middle of the day, and so we travelled along until after sunset, when we doubled back, and made in the direction of the farm described in the letter.

About four o'clock in the afternoon we passed a hut. Of course every one, knowing we were in search of the Kellys, came out to see us. One of my men drew my attention to a man standing watching us, and told me he was one of the principal spies of the Kellys. I replied, " Well, he can never guess where we are going, for we have the Warby Ranges between us and the spot we are making for." We passed on, and thought nothing more of him. We got into camp about eight o'clock, tied our horses up, and after having some water, bread, and beef, laid down until one o'clock in the morning. As the men got out of their hammocks, Lawless cried out, "I say, Mr. Hare, I think some of these hammocks will be for sale to-night." He meant by that that some of us would be shot, as all felt convinced we were going to meet the outlaws that morning.

The men were all in great spirits. We had to cross the railway gates at Glenrowan. We often found great difficulty in crossing the railway, for many of the gate-keepers were in league with the friends of the Kelly gang. The keeper required a lot of calling before he got up. We then struck across the bush until we were compelled to get on to the roads; when amongst the farm-houses we had to travel very quietly to avoid alarming the occupants, for we looked upon every one as a sympathizer of the outlaws. After travelling about four hours, the constable who undertook to take us to the farm referred to, said he thought we were near the place, so we all dismounted and left our horses on the road in charge of one of the party. The remainder approached the house carefully, and we got in front of it just half an hour before daybreak. I told my sergeant, with three of the men, to take up his position at the back of the house, and that I would, when it was clear daylight, put my hat on my rifle as a sign for him to approach. I remained on the spot with three men for about half an hour. They were strung up to such a pitch that I thought I should hardly be able to restrain them from rushing ahead of me.

At the appointed time I gave the signal, and we started for the house. We had to pass a window before getting to the door, and in doing so one of the men stepped in front of me. He told me afterwards that he thought a shot would have been fired out of the window, and he wanted to get between me and it. We went to the door and listened, but all was silent within. I knocked, and a man inside called out, "Who's there?" I replied, "Police; open the door." After a few seconds he did so. I said, "Have you any strangers in your house?" He said, "I have." I suppose our appearance there frightened the life out of him, for he turned deadly pale; but the moment he said there were strangers inside we all rushed into the house and into every room in the building. I said to the farmer, "Let me see the strangers," and out came the individual whom we had passed the previous evening, the greatest sympathizer Kelly had. I asked him what brought him there. He said he came over to see his friend and spend the night with him.

We saw at once our chance was gone. I never could learn whether this man, upon seeing us pass the previous evening, had gone over to warn the Kellys to be on the look-out. We searched the haystack, outbuildings, and every place that we could think of, but all to no purpose. There was nothing to be done but to return to the camp a disappointed crew. I don't think I ever saw the men so down-hearted. Whilst returning, I thought I would try to raise their spirits, and so I took them across country. We got in amongst the fences, and there was a good deal of jumping to do to get back to camp. One of the men had a narrow escape of falling off, his horse blundering over a fence. He landed on its ears, and had the greatest difficulty in getting back to his saddle. This little incident put the men in good humour again. We had our breakfast, turned the horses loose, and got into our hammocks, where we remained all that day, both men and horses requiring rest. Next day we took a turn in the Warby Ranges, and made back to Benalla.

I had a great many trips with my party in the Warby Ranges. I was told by a sergeant of police, who ought to have known better, that I could search these ranges thoroughly in a couple of days. However, after a month's experience, I found every day new hiding-places where the outlaws could conceal themselves. I had a splendid lot of fellows in my party. My right-hand man was Mayes, who acted as my sergeant; next to him was Mills, and the others were Lawless, Faulkner, Barry, O'Loughlin, and Kirkham. They were all men who belonged to my own district, and had served under me for years. There was not a weak spot in any of them. I felt that I could at any moment have said, "I think the outlaws are in that cave, go and pull them out," and they would have been proud to have been selected for the purpose. No work was too much for them, day or night, and I never heard a grumble. Lawless and Faulkner were equal to any bush-riders in the world, and I often wished that they might have a chance of showing whether they or the Kellys were the best men on horseback. Johnstone was another of my men, but he was not always with me. He also was a magnificent rider, but he required some restraint, being both wild and reckless, and inclined to lose his head.

Generally speaking, we had two pack-horses to carry our provisions and rugs, enough to last us eight or ten days; after that the men required a spell in barracks, for our life was a very hard one, sleeping in the open without tent or fire, living on potted beef, and biscuit, and sardines. Bushmen think nothing of camping out for months, but ask any of them in the winter months to camp out without a fire, and see how long they will stand it. I remember once, when I was searching the mountains at the head of the Broken river, the weather was terribly cold, and the men were getting very downhearted at not having any luck. Mayes came to me and asked me to let the men have a fire for one night, as they were very low-spirited, and were feeling the cold terribly. He said, "I am sure if we could get to some quiet spot in the mountains you could let us have one good warm, and we shall be all right to-morrow." I agreed, and took them to a most retired gully, and told them they might light a fire that night. They were so surprised, it acted like magic on them. They selected a large hollow tree, set fire to it, and there was a grand blaze. They heaped up wood all round, and sat all night enjoying themselves.

After I had had a good warm I took my hammock and went about a hundred yards from them, and kept, as it were, watch over them, because I never knew when the Kellys might have crept on us, and without any difficulty they might have shot the whole of the men standing round the fire; so I thought if they were attacked I could have assisted them. First of all they made bets as to how long it would be before the tree would fall; one said two hours, another three, and so on. Then they began to bet how many native bears there would be in the tree when it fell, then who would catch the first opossum, and so they went on all night, like a lot of school-boys out for a holiday.

The next day they were quite different men, and we had several adventures, such as one of the pack-horses rolling down a precipice. I was riding ahead, and hearing a terrible noise, looked round and saw that one of the pack-horses had slipped and fallen over the cliff. It was rolling down, turning over and over like a barrel, the stones and rattling of the pack on his back making such a noise that I thought half the men were over. The track was too narrow to turn my horse round, but I jumped off and looked over the embankment, and there I saw the poor old horse lying on his side eating grass. I expected to see him smashed to pieces. We had to work our way down to the bottom, take off the pack, and lead the horse a mile or two round before we got him to where the rest were. Strange to say, with the exception of a few cuts, the horse was all right, but this accident caused a delay of two hours.

A BAD NIGHT.

The tracks in the mountains are made by the wild cattle, and I am sure I often thought it a marvel that we did not roll down the sidlings we crossed. One night we spent a terrible time. We had arrived at the foot of a steep mountain, and I told the men to camp there, and fixed the spot where my hammock was to be slung. I then took three men with me and ascended the mountain. It was a fearfully wild place. I went up to see if I could observe any signs of fire in the distance. We stayed on the top of the mountain for an hour or two, and then descended; but we had a terrible job to get back with our rifles in our hands. It was pitch dark, and the difficulty of our position caused much amusement. Every now and then one of us would come bump up against a rock, and we would be calling to each other to ascertain whether we were keeping together, and we were very doubtful whether we should find the spot where the other men were camped. However, I had taken particular notice of the hills as I went up, and if there is one thing I am proud of being able to do more than another, it is being able to find my way about the bush. I have been thirty years knocking about the country, and I only once lost myself, and had to stay out all night, and that was under very excep tional circumstances.

We got to the camp, had some tucker, and I jumped into my hammock, which had been slung between two saplings, when two or three native bears began to sing out in a most piteous manner, like children crying. I stood this for a short time, and then called out to one of the men to cut the tree down, so as to get rid of the bears. He did so, and I fastened my hammock to the stump of the tree, and fell asleep. When I awoke in the morning my rug was frozen, the country round was perfectly white with frost, and the men told me the running water in the creek close by was frozen.

One night in the Warby Ranges is forcibly fixed in my mind. We were in one of the most favourite resorts of the outlaws, and were searching a side of the mountain. The men were stationed at equal distances from one another. I was very anxious to search all the gullies leading up the mountain, so I took the lower position myself, the men being all above me. They searched every nook and corner, behind all the rocks, the scrub, and any place in which a man could hide.

As I was riding along I saw a newspaper a day or two old folded up and stuck between two rocks. It had a long article abusing the police for not capturing the Kellys, and had evidently been put there for the outlaws' perusal. Not far from this I found a track leading up a gully in the mountains. I looked up, and saw Lawless about 100 yards above me, and beckoned to him to come to me, which he did. I showed him the track into the gully. He said, "What shall we do?" I told him we had better search it. We got off our horses, tied them to a tree, and walked up the gully. I took one side and Lawless the other. We were not more than eighty yards apart.

Shortly afterwards I saw Lawless trying to attract my attention; he beckoned to me to come to him; I did so. When I got near he pointed downwards, as if there was something beneath the rock he was standing on. He had his rifle in position to fire at a moment's notice. I could not understand what he meant or what he had seen. He remained where he was, and I went round to the front of the rock he was standing on. He said when he jumped on the rock he felt something move it, and heard a noise as if some one was running underneath it. I went close up to the opening, and there I saw a large wombat in the hole. I told him what was there, and his countenance changed in a moment. When I first came up to him his eyes were starting out of his head with excitement, and he said, "I thought we had them at last."

We continued our search, but as usual, there was nothing to be seen. We got on our horses and rode about the place until about five o'clock, when we came across a nice paddock, and decided upon turning our horses into it and camping for the night. We had fixed the different spots for our hammocks, and were just going to our meal, when one of the men called me, and pointed out the tracks of fresh horse foot-prints going into the mountains from the direction of the lowlands. The tracks appeared to be an hour or two old. We were considering what we should do, and sat down in the usual manner away from each other with our rifles beside us, when all of a sudden every man jumped to his feet and called out, "Look out, sir, they are coming straight for us." I stood up and saw four men riding towards us as hard as their horses could go. It was the habit of the Kellys to ride like demons through the country.

My whole party rushed to a brush fence and got behind it; I followed them, and the men came straight for us. When they were within a few yards we all jumped up and confronted them. They were not the outlaws, but were well-known spies of theirs. Directly we stopped them they began to slang and chaff us. Sergeant Mayes turned upon them in the most indignant manner, and asked if they knew who they were speaking to. Mayes asked me if he might arrest them, as he felt sure the outlaws were close by.

I consented, and told him the better plan would be for him to take three of our men to the house from whence these men had come, and put the four sympathizers in it, and allow no person to leave the place that night. I and the three other men would watch the pass leading into the mountains. Mayes, Lawless, Faulkner, and O'Loughlin went off, leaving three men with me. They proceeded towards the house, which was the same place where the outlaws had their breakfast after riding through Wangaratta, shortly after the murders.

As the party approached, all the occupants came to the door, evidently thinking the four strangers were the Kelly gang, and there appeared to be great rejoicing over the prospect of their calling there, but as the party got closer, and were recognized as policemen, they all beat a retreat into the house. Lawless, who was a small man, not at all unlike Steve Hart in figure and appearance, saw a person walking in the garden, and directly he caught sight of him the man appeared to vanish out of his sight. Lawless followed him, and when he got near, the man called out, "Is that you, Steve?" Lawless replied, "No." He said, "Then it must be his brother." Lawless replied, "It is neither." The man then took a good look at Lawless and said, "I beg your pardon, I thought you were some one else." Lawless said, "Who did you take me for?" He replied, "Some one we expected to-night." Lawless at once reported this conversation to Mayes, who sent him to where they had left me, and Lawless informed me of all that had passed between him and the stranger. I at once decided to watch the place with my three men. About a mile from the house there was a good stable, with abundance of feed in it, which was evidently left there for the outlaws. Mayes had told the inmates of the house they were not to come out during the night, as he and his men intended keeping watch over the place, and they might be mistaken for some one else, and shot. When I reached the house they appeared to be very happy inside; they kept dancing half the night, and I believe this was a sign for the outlaws, if they were about, to keep away.

There we remained without covering of any kind until daylight. The night was bitterly cold, and I, being in the most exposed place, became nearly frozen. About two o'clock in the morning I had a consultation with Mayes, and we decided to send a man into Wangaratta to bring out four additional constables to keep watch, whilst my party tried to pick up the tracks we had seen the evening before, leading into the mountains. I sent Faulkner with another man to Wangaratta, at about four o'clock in the morning; he returned with the four men. On his arrival, I met him near the house, and directly I approached him he sheered off from me, and said, "Who are you?" I said, "Don't you know me?" When he heard my voice, he replied, "Is that you, Mr. Hare? You are so white with the frost I did not know you." I gave orders to Sergeant Kelly, who was in charge of the fresh men, to guard the house, and to allow no person to leave until I communicated with him. I told him on no account to allow any signals to be put out, especially any sheet to be thrown over a bush in the garden, this being a well-known sign of the Kellys as a warning not to approach the house. Sergeant Kelly afterwards told me, directly the people of the house had finished breakfast, one of the girls brought out a table-cloth, shook it on the verandah, and then threw it over a bush in the garden. He removed it at once.

At daybreak I and my party went to the pass in

the mountains, where we had left all our packs and provisions. We had some breakfast, and started off immediately to follow the tracks. I had no black tracker with me, but I had an excellent man named Bellis; he was one of the special men engaged by the police, who knew the country. He was a capital bushman, a good shot, a fair tracker, and a thoroughly trustworthy man. We took our horses with us. Bellis and several of the men picked up the tracks, whilst the others followed with the horses. For a mile or so the tracks were very distinct, but after some distance they appeared to separate, going in different directions. Some of the men fancied they heard voices ahead, and asked me to allow them to run over, as they felt certain the outlaws were quite near. I could hear no voices, but two or three of the men said they did. There was a thick clump of scrub in the direction where the men thought they heard the voices, so I beckoned to them to join together, and we rushed towards the scrub and surrounded it. We searched it thoroughly, but could find no trace of anybody being there. The men were much excited from want of sleep, and they appeared hardly to know what they were doing, so I made them have a rest. Afterwards we went back to pick up the tracks again, but were unable to do so. We searched the mountains until evening, and then made back to the spot where we had left our packs.

Next day we started off into the hills. I sent a man from the house to Senior-constable Kelly, and told him to withdraw his men into the mountains, so as to keep watch over the house, and to remain as long as his provisions would last. We searched all the day without finding any signs of the outlaws. We camped that night at the foot of a steep mountain, and were starting off next morning when Bellis drew my attention to what we all thought were the heads of four men looking over the hill at us. Without a moment's consideration, the whole party started to get up the hill as fast as they could. It was a difficult job for the horses, but we urged them on. The only things we could see were four goats feeding quietly. We looked for traces of men, but could find none, and so came to the conclusion that we must have mistaken the goats for four men looking down on us. I myself had grave doubts, and still think they were men. There was a high point of the mountain in front of us, which we next proceeded to search.

As my horse was carrying twenty stone, when I got on the top of the hill I dismounted and walked over to some shelving rocks. There I found the foot-marks of a man on the green moss, as if done that morning. I went back to meet my men, and showed the foot-marks to them, and after we had followed the tracks for some distance we came across a lot of stones recently moved, the earth being quite fresh. The stones were up on end, all pointing in one direction, and that was to another high hill three or four miles off. We lost the tracks in the rocky ground, so decided to try our luck on the other hill. We kept some distance apart from each other, making for the steep ground in front of us. After a most tedious ascent we reached the top, at least four of us did, and, strange to relate, here we found the stones stuck up on end just as we had found them on the other hill. We were greatly puzzled at this, and while we were talking over the matter one of the men saw a person at the foot of the hill on horseback, riding along at a good pace. I sent a man after him to see who he was, and he overtook him as he was making for the mountain. The man I had sent immediately beckoned to me to come down, and appeared to be very excited. We all made down the hill as fast as we could.

This person was a well-known squatter living close by, who had often aided the police when in want of assistance. He told me that when he was in the mountains the previous day looking for some sheep, he saw a tent erected in a retired spot, and it must only recently have been put there. I asked him if he would take us to it. He said "Certainly." I collected all my men, and off we started, following our leader. After riding some four or five miles the tent was pointed out. We dismounted and surrounded it, and rushed down on it, only to meet with another disappointment. The tent was quite empty. We searched all round the place, and found tracks of shod horses where the animals had been feeding. We retired from the tent and slept that night near the squatter's homestead, and I dined with him, but slept with my men.

Next morning at daylight we saddled our horses and made back to the tent we had searched the previous evening. We again crept down, thinking the occupants, if any, might be asleep; but it was still empty. Some time afterwards I heard the tent belonged to a party of men engaged collecting honey, who are known as "bee men." Many of them were sympathizers of the outlaws, and used to leave horse-feed and provisions in their tents for them. We continued searching for three or four days after this, but nothing of any interest transpired.

We were constantly receiving information that the outlaws were likely to be hiding amongst their friends on the low land below Euroa, where they were known to have several cousins who did not bear very good characters. Captain Standish suggested that I should again take a trip down there. I had made several trips in those parts before, but some fresh information supplied to us was to the effect that they were hiding in the flat country. I started off with my party and a black-fellow called Moses. He was a Queensland man, and a capital tracker. He had been with me on several occasions before. We searched about the country, but could hear nothing of the outlaws.

One morning we made an early start to search a place belonging to a connection of the Kellys. We left our pack-horses behind us, and also our bedding and provisions, intending to go across country, getting over the fences the best way we could. After riding two or three hours we came across a stiff fence, and there was no way of getting over except to jump it. The men went over it with the greatest ease, but when I brought my horse up he baulked. I turned him round and put him at it again, and he made a tremendous spring and got over. Something gave way in my back, just above my right hip, and the agony I went through that day was beyond anything I ever experienced.

A most amusing incident occurred on this day. We had received information that the outlaws were amongst their relations, and during the day they occupied a very large haystack, near the house of one of their relatives. I was in great agony when I reached this place; still the description we had received of the premises was so accurate that we made straight for the stack, and much to my astonishment found a chamber or passage leading into it. We all dismounted from our horses, and I called for a volunteer to creep inside and see what was in it. Every man begged to be allowed to explore it, and I selected Johnstone. He disappeared in a moment, but very soon reappeared, coming out a good deal faster than he went in. He said, "I heard some noise in the stack, and I came back to tell you to keep a sharp look-out all round." I started him back, and told him to turn the fellows out, and in he went again; but he had hardly been away twenty seconds when out he came again like a flash of lightning. I said, "What is the matter?" He replied, "Lor, sir, there is an old sow in there with a lot of young ones, and she *did* go for me; it was as much as I could do to keep clear of her." The old pig came out shortly afterwards, and we all had a good laugh.

We had information about another place further on, but I was unable to proceed. I lay down in the bush in great pain, and sent the men to search the locality; and on their return they picked me up, and we returned to where we had left the camp in the morning, a distance of about twenty-five miles.

Next morning I was better, and the men got a buggy for me, and I drove myself into Euroa. I do not to this day know what was the matter with me, or the cause of the pain I suffered. The party I left behind in charge of Senior-constable Johnstone remained out for five or six days, and then returned to Benalla. On my arrival at Benalla I told Captain Standish that the hardships I had gone through had affected my constitution, and I was not fit to go out with the search party again, and I wished him to relieve me, as I had then been camping out for eight or nine months. He promised to do so, and ordered the inspecting superintendent to come up and take over charge of the business. I got a week's leave, and remained quietly at Benalla.

CHAPTER X.

Black Trackers—Again in Charge with *carte blanche*—Aaron Sherritt's Doom—The Beginning of the End—Glenrowan—Sticking up the Hotel—Bracken's Escape—The Police on the Alert — A Dangerous Journey — Mr. Curnow's Adventure.

BEFORE I close this part of my narrative I wish to say that I have not given a hundredth part of what actually took place during the time I was searching for the outlaws. I felt sure, sooner or later, one of the different parties who were out in search of them would drop across them, as the outlaws had always to be on the alert, never knowing when a party would be on them. Ned Kelly said after his capture, the hardest part of their life was the constantly keeping guard for fear of surprise. They were dreadfully afraid of the black trackers—I mean the men that came from Queensland—I was told it was marvellous how these men could follow a track across the bush. I was out on two occasions with them, but I did not see anything particularly striking about them, but other Victorian officers spoke in the highest terms of their wonderful skill in tracking.

When Moses was with me I saw him do a fine piece of tracking. We were on a flat at the back of Warby's Ranges, and after lunch started to search a range in the mountains, leaving our packs at the camp, and a man in charge. We had been searching several hills, and about half an hour before sunset one of the men drew my attention to some tracks of horses coming from the Wangaratta side of the range. I called Moses and showed them to him. He dismounted, looked about, and said they were from horse tracks about four days old, three big horses and one small one; he pointed in the direction they were going. It was exactly in the opposite direction to where our camp was. He said, "Shall I follow them?" I replied, "Yes." He took some cartridges out of his belt and put one in his rifle, and without saying another word, off he galloped as hard as he could go across country, we all following him. We went for about five or six miles. Suddenly Moses pulled up, and we found ourselves on the cross road running from Wangaratta to Yarrawonga. Moses said, "The tracks have gone into this dusty road, and I can't follow them any further." I replied, "Surely you have not been on the tracks all the while." He said, "Oh, yes; I will show you." He got off his horse and showed me the four tracks—three large horses and one small one. He then galloped up one side of the cross road and back the other, to see if the tracks crossed either the one side or the other, but without any result. We then returned to our camp. We were without coats, it was bitterly cold, and we had nine or ten miles to ride.

Next morning we started to try and pick up the tracks again, and I suggested we should work back to see where they came from. We did so, and found they were coming from the direction of a sympathizer's house which we had surrounded a few nights before. We rode on for about a mile, and suddenly Moses pulled up, and said, "They have been camping here." I could see no signs of anything. I said, "How do you know?" He replied, "One saddle been there," pointing to a spot, "another there, and there." I dismounted and could see no signs of anything. We searched about and found where a small fire had been made. Searching further he found under some rocks, where the black fellow had noticed the stones had been removed, the identical tins which we had given

Sergeant Kelly when I directed him to take up his position in the mountain overlooking the house. I afterwards ascertained that it was just four days before we were there, that Sergeant Kelly had left this camp and gone the road Moses had followed the previous evening. I have given this story just to show the wonderful powers these blacks have in following tracks.

In addition to going out in search parties, I had a number of agents always working for me, but I felt the information they gave was of little use. They would tell us the outlaws were seen at some distant place, and what they intended doing, but all this information was of little service to us, beyond letting us know they were in the country. This we had no doubt of, and I often asked Sherritt if there was any chance of them leaving the district, and he scorned the idea. He said, "Most decidedly they can never leave, and the day they attempt to do so they will be captured." I never could understand why they did not separate and make for Queensland as swagmen; but Sherritt was quite right; they never did leave, beyond going across the Murray, where they had many friends, and they were always within a day or two's ride of their own relations. They never had horses with them, except when they went on some raid; otherwise we must some time or other have come across their tracks. They could not have kept their horses out of sight. I was told that on two or three occasions I and my party nearly surprised them, and that once they had to take refuge in the head of a fallen tree to escape us.

When the inspecting superintendent relieved me he adopted a different system to mine. He did away with all search parties, and depended entirely on agents, thinking he might lead the outlaws to believe that he was under the impression they had left the colony, and thus beget a feeling of security which might lead them to become careless about their movements. He had some reliable agents, who were giving him information of all the movements of the outlaws. Our two systems were entirely different. I thought mine was the best, the inspecting superintendent thought otherwise, and he begged to be allowed to continue carrying out his plans. The press throughout the colony was calling out about the disgraceful conduct of the police in not capturing the offenders. A change of Ministry having taken place about this time, the Government were determined to try some other measures to effect the arrest of the bushrangers.

One morning Captain Standish told me that Mr. Ramsay, the chief secretary, had decided I was to relieve the inspecting superintendent, and take charge of affairs again at Benalla. I protested, and told him I had already tried my hand and failed, and that there were many officers in the force senior to me who should have a trial. He replied: " The Government have decided upon your going, and you must go." I saw the chief secretary on the subject, and his reply was, " Mr. Hare, the Cabinet have decided that you are to take charge of affairs at Benalla. They have the utmost confidence in your discretion, we give you *carte blanche* to do whatever you think desirable, you are to consider yourself independent of all control, and anything you do the Government will bear you out in." I told Mr. Ramsay that I felt very much flattered at the confidence reposed in me, and that I was ready to start at once.

In the meantime the inspecting superintendent, having received orders to hand over the charge of affairs to me, came at once to Melbourne, and saw Mr. Ramsay. He told the chief secretary he felt sure if left in the district a short time longer, he would without doubt capture the outlaws. He begged to be allowed to remain a little while, and Mr.

Ramsay gave him another month. He went back to Benalla, and did everything in his power to effect a capture, but all to no purpose—and I was compelled to go back to Benalla, very much against my inclination, on 1st June 1880.

I first began to find out what had been going on during my absence from the district. I saw some of the agents who had been employed by the inspecting superintendent, and got them to remain in my employ. I then took steps to remove the trackers, as I had informed Mr. Ramsay, it was said that as long as they were in the district the outlaws would not show out, and I was anxious they should do something, as it would give us a better opportunity of falling across them. Besides, the Queensland authorities wanted their trackers back, as they belonged to their force of native police, and the officer in charge was anxious to return also. I arranged with Captain Standish they should leave as soon as they could conveniently do so.

After I had found out all I could concerning the movements of the outlaws at Benalla, I started off to Beechworth and saw Aaron Sherritt. I found he had married during my absence, and his family and his wife's relations did not get on together, as she was a Roman Catholic and he a Protestant, and his family were vexed with him for marrying. Aaron had taken a cottage on the road from Beechworth to Eldorado near Woolshed, where he and his wife resided. I had a long interview with him, finding out all that had taken place during my absence, and the different interviews he had had with the outlaws whilst I was away from the district. He expressed himself very pleased at my return, and told me he did not get on as well with the inspecting superintendent as he did with me, and he would set to work with fresh zeal and endeavour to find out where the outlaws were to be found. He told me that a fortnight ago they were at his mother's house looking for his brother Jack, whom they wanted to join them, and four constables had been sent to his house in hopes that they might call on him; but when the inspecting superintendent was leaving the district, these men had been removed, and he was of opinion that it would be as well to send them back.

I ordered them back, and directed that they should stay indoors all day and watch Mrs. Byrne's house by night, as Aaron lived about three-quarters of a mile from her. I also made arrangements to have the Harts' house watched from Wangaratta, and for a party to watch Kelly's house from Glenrowan.

The orders to the men were, that after dark every night they were to leave their abode singly, and walk away to the watching-place, so that if any of them should be met, no notice would be taken of a man walking alone. They were to take up their positions within view of the houses, but not near enough for the inmates to discover their whereabouts.

I kept moving about and working hard. Rumours were coming in from all directions that the sympathizers were very active, that something was about to happen. Old Mrs. Byrne was very jubilant, and she told a person—who repeated it to me—that the gang was about to do something that would astonish not only the colony, but the whole world.

Horses were reported as being stolen in several directions, all supposed to be by the gang. Constable Bracken, who was in charge at Glenrowan, reported that the four men who had been watching Kelly's house were completely knocked up, being out night after night in the wet, and asked me to let them be sent to Benalla to recruit themselves for a few days. I consented, but I had no other men to replace them. I paid another visit to Beechworth, saw Detective Ward, and told him I was not at all satisfied with the way the men were conducting things at Aaron's house.

Two or three reports came to hand, informing me that Paddy Byrne had saddled his horse at his mother's place at two o'clock in the morning, and started off into the ranges, and instead of the men accompanying Aaron to endeavour to follow him, they let him go alone. I decided to go down that night to visit the party at Woolshed. Ward and I started away from Beechworth about eight o'clock, and reached Aaron's house about 9.30. I stood in the road whilst Ward went to the house to find out from Aaron's wife where the men were to be found, as they should have been out watching. We found one of the men at the hut, and he told us the others were away with Aaron watching Mrs. Byrne's house. I left Ward at the hut, and got this constable to show me where the men were watching. He purposely lost his way, and kept me fully an hour going one mile. I believe he kept me all this while in the bush to gain time for the men to take up their positions, as it turned out that none of the men were watching Mrs. Byrne's house but Aaron.

When I got to the watching-place I met the constable who was in charge of the party. I asked him why he had left one constable behind at Aaron's house? His reply was, "That man has deceived you, Mr. Hare; we were all of us at Aaron's house when you called with Ward," he said. "I was collecting wood on the hills—Aaron alone was watching." I severely reprimanded the constable for misleading me. I then spoke to the constable in charge about matters in general. He appeared to be a smart, intelligent man. I asked if he had made up his mind what he would do if the outlaws came to Mrs. Byrne's. He said: "I would shoot the lot of them if Aaron said they were the men." I told him to be careful not to make a mistake and shoot any one else. I left them, and Aaron walked back with me to his house to pilot me across the diggings.

No sooner did he get within sight of his house than he said, "You can't go wrong; there is the house. I will return, as I don't like leaving the men there alone." I saw he was just as zealous as ever. I thought all this zeal might have been put on to deceive me, but I listened to his footsteps making back as fast as he could. I thought after he had let me go he would probably return to his hut for a cup of tea, as the night was bitterly cold, and he was dressed as usual, with a white shirt, trousers, and boots. I sat there fully half an hour, but I heard no sign of his returning. I went to the hut, picked up Ward and my horse, and rode back to Beechworth, telling Ward I was convinced that the men at Sherritt's house were not working as they should, and that I had decided I would remove them and send others in their place as soon as I could arrange to do so. Exactly at that time on the following Saturday Aaron was shot, and two of the outlaws were guarding his place for some hours afterwards.

On Saturday evening, the 26th June, about nine o'clock, a man named Antone Wicks, a German, who lived about a quarter of a mile from Aaron Sherritt's house, was stuck up by Joe Byrne and Dan Kelly. He was handcuffed by the outlaws, and made to accompany them to Sherritt's house. He was told to call Aaron out, and say he had lost his way, and ask him to put him on the road, as it was quite dark. When the three arrived at Aaron's house Wicks knocked at the door; Aaron said, "Who is there?" The German replied, "It is Antone Wicks, he has lost his way." Aaron opened the door, and Wicks said, "Come and show me the way." Aaron said, "Who is that?" at the same moment stepping out of his door. Joe Byrne jumped forward and fired at him. He retreated to the middle of the room, and Byrne stood in the doorway and fired a second shot, and Aaron dropped down dead without saying a word. It

AARON SHERRITT'S DOOM. 239

is commonly believed that Ned Kelly was present at the shooting of Sherritt, but Wicks stated that only Byrne and Dan Kelly were there; they kept him handcuffed all the while they remained at Sherritt's house.

It might be as well to explain why they took Wicks up to Aaron's house to call him out. The outlaws may have heard voices in Aaron's house, and thought that if they called him outside his door their voices would have been recognized by him, and he would have been on his guard, so they got Wicks, who lived close by Aaron, to call him.

Whilst all this was going on at Woolshed, Ned Kelly and Hart were busy elsewhere. About 2.20 o'clock on Sunday morning 27th June, a railway line repairer, named Reardon, was awakened by Ned Kelly and Hart at Glenrowan, and told to get up and dress himself. Kelly presented a revolver at his head, and told him he wanted him and a man named Sullivan, also a line repairer, to go and pull up the rails. He said, "We were at Beechworth last night, and killed several people. I expect a special train will be sent from Benalla with a number of police and black trackers, and I am going to kill the lot." Reardon begged

Kelly not to take him, as he had a wife and large family. Kelly replied, "You must come, or I will shoot you." Kelly told him to pick up the tools he required. Kelly, Hart, Reardon, and some other workmen walked along the line to a place about half a mile away from Glenrowan, where there was a steep embankment with a fall on each side of about twenty or thirty feet. Hart pointed out the rails to be taken up, and Reardon and the others took up two rails. They were a considerable time about it, and Kelly found fault with them for not being quicker, and threatened to tickle some of them with his revolver if they did not hurry up. When this was done they all walked back to Glenrowan, and were marched into Mrs. Jones's hotel, and were kept prisoners there.

It is not positively known at what hour Joe Byrne and Steve Hart appeared on the scene, but it was some time in the morning. Throughout the day the four outlaws took possession of the township. They kept watching for persons passing Mrs. Jones's hotel, and they would call upon them to "bail up," and march them off to the hotel, which for the time being was converted into a prison-house by the outlaws. By the evening they had captured sixty-two people. Amongst

STEVE HART.

those thus detained was Constable Bracken, an excellent ex-constable, who rejoined the force for the express purpose of assisting in the capture of the Kelly gang. He was a clever, shrewd, careful, quiet man. Young Reynolds, the son of a neighbour, came to the police station about eight or nine o'clock on Sunday night, and called Bracken to come outside to his father, who wanted him. The object in getting Reynolds to call Bracken, was to prevent the constable from recognizing the outlaw's voice, so the boy, who lived near the police station, was made to call him.

It was the habit of constables, when called by any one during the night, not to show themselves unless they had their revolvers in their hands. Bracken, hearing young Reynolds' voice, got up without taking this precaution; being unwell, he had gone to bed early. The moment he opened his door, which led into the yard, Ned Kelly, who was standing beside the boy, covered him with his revolver, and ordered him back into the house. One of the other outlaws was also present. Kelly at the time had his armour on, with a waterproof coat over all. They made Bracken dress himself, he being the only constable at the station, and told his wife that she was to remain in the barracks,

R

and, if she gave information to any one, or answered any call during the night, they would shoot her husband. Mrs. Bracken said she looked out of her window two or three times during the night, and saw men watching her house. This may have been fancy or fear on her part. Bracken was marched off to Jones's hotel, and found sixty-two prisoners there. Dancing was going on, and everybody appeared in great spirits. Of course, amongst these sixty-two prisoners there were several of the Kellys' sympathizers, who, if a rush had been contemplated, would have given the gang warning. When Bracken was admitted into the room the doors were locked, so that nobody could leave. Dan Kelly had charge of the key which opened the front door, and Bracken kept watching him.

About ten or eleven o'clock at night Dan Kelly commenced to dance, and before doing so he put the key on a mantel-piece. Bracken sidled towards the fire-place, and taking the key, slipped it down his boot unobserved by any one. The dancing was kept up with great spirit until some one called out, "The train is approaching!" The outlaws at once went into an adjoining room and began to put on their armour, but no one knew what they were doing. About ten minutes afterwards the train stopped, and there was great excitement. Bracken saw his chance of escape. He took the key from his boot, opened the front door, and ran towards the railway station. The first thing the Kellys did when they came out of the side room was to look for Bracken, but they could not find him, and appeared very much annoyed.

About one o'clock on Sunday afternoon, 27th June, a messenger was sent to my hotel in Benalla, who told me that there was an important message for me at the telegraph office. I went there, and found that intelligence had come that Aaron Sherritt had been shot at his own house at nine o'clock the previous night by the outlaws. I at once sent a wire to Captain Standish, telling him of the circumstances, and requesting him to send the black trackers back to Benalla at once, as they had left for Melbourne on the previous Friday.

Captain Standish was out of town when the telegram arrived, and it did not reach him till about five in the afternoon. He then at once placed himself in communication with Mr. Ramsay, the chief secretary, and, strange to say, sent me a wire that he would send the trackers up by an early train next morning. I replied, "If they are not sent up by a special train to-night, they need not come at all."

In the meantime Mr. Ramsay called on the Minister of Railways, and arranged to have a "special" ready to take the trackers back to Benalla, and they left town about eight or nine o'clock that night, and were to reach Benalla about 12.30 A.M. The officer in charge of the district and myself remained all the afternoon at the telegraph office, and I can never forget the assistance rendered me during that trying afternoon by that officer. Unfortunately, it being Sunday, many of the operators were away from their offices. We called as many as we could, and had to engage private individuals to convey on horseback the intelligence to others, directing them to be ready for any emergency that might happen. We felt sure that something of importance would follow such a deed, but had no idea when or where it would take place, so that every possible precaution had to be taken.

We sent to the railway station and ordered a special train to be ready in case the trackers were not coming up that night, and I arranged to take a party of men from Benalla to Beechworth. Unfortunately, none of my old men were there, but still I had a very good lot. I had also two of our own black trackers, "Moses" and "Spider," both Queensland men, but they did not come specially

THE START FROM BENALLA. 245

to Victoria as trackers. I kept them, and would have taken them had the others not been sent back to me; and we also arranged, in the event of anything happening during my absence, to have a party of men ready to start off at a moment's notice.

We got a wire that the trackers would leave Melbourne that night, and so we decided to keep the special engine that was ready for us to act as a pilot to our train. Everything was in order to start off directly the men arrived. My plans were as follows:—The train with my own men, horses, and trackers would reach Beechworth about four o'clock in the morning (Monday); we would get our horses out directly we arrived, and start off to Sherritt's house, put the trackers on the outlaws' tracks, and endeavour to follow them.

We had made no other plans beyond these. In my own mind I felt convinced we should never reach Beechworth, but I told no one of my convictions. About ten o'clock I lay down to get an hour's sleep, and at midnight had all the horses and baggage put in the train, so that we could start off directly the trackers arrived. They reached Benalla a little after one, having had some delay on the road in consequence of having run through some gates, which flew up and broke the brakes.

It was decided by the railway authorities at Benalla that the engine that came from Melbourne should act as pilot. I had a consultation with the two engine-drivers before we started, telling them to be on the alert and keep a good look-out, as I felt sure either the rails would be pulled up, or something would happen before we got to Beechworth. The driver of the Benalla engine asked me to let a constable stand on the side-plate in front so as to keep a good look-out. I selected Constable Barry for this post. He was to fasten a strap round the brass rod which runs along the engine, and to put his arm through that to hold on by. It was afterwards stated that I had made him sit on the buffers. However, the driver of the pilot engine dispensed with his services, so Barry was not put in this dangerous position. I told the driver of my train on no account to let the pilot get more than a hundred yards away from him, and consulted the two drivers as to the most probable place for the rails to be interfered with. They fixed on the very spot where the rails were taken up. I told them to be very careful in going down the hill indicated. It was arranged we were not to stop between Benalla and Wangaratta, there being no occasion for doing so.

We left Benalla a little before two o'clock. The

train from Melbourne had brought up the officer in charge of the five trackers, and five reporters connected with the Melbourne papers. The officer in charge of the trackers having recently been married, we allowed his wife and sister to accompany him in the train, intending that they should remain at Beechworth while he followed the tracks of the outlaws. I got into the compartment with the officer and the ladies, the reporters having a compartment to themselves, and the constables another. I had put my rifle on the rack of the carriage, and was just arranging to lie down and have a sleep, when the engine gave a whistle, and stopped. I jumped up, put my head out of the window, and saw the three red lights of the pilot just ahead of us. I loaded my rifle, jumped out of the train, and met the guard of the pilot coming towards me. We were then about a mile from Glenrowan. He told me that they had seen a red light on the line, and pulling up to ascertain what it was, found a man, who said he was the schoolmaster, and stated that the Kelly gang had pulled up the line of rails, and he told the driver he must be very careful. This person then ran away, notwithstanding that the driver begged him to see me before he left. They told him I was in the train behind; but he said no, he had to return to his wife, and ran off. It afterwards turned out the man was Mr. Curnow, the local schoolmaster, who, having no lamp by which to stop the train, got a red scarf and held a candle behind it when he heard the train approaching, but, having left his wife alone, he hurried back for fear some of the gang might see him.

After the guard of the pilot had related this story to me, I called four of my men, and putting two on each side of the line, we walked towards the engine. The driver told me the same story as the guard. I considered for a moment what was best to be done, consulting with my men, and thinking that the information given by the person representing himself as a schoolmaster was a ruse, especially as Glenrowan was only about three miles from Kelly's house, I returned to my train (they were about 150 yards apart), and told those who were in the train to be prepared for any emergency, as I could not say what might happen. I put my senior constable with three men on the tender belonging to the train engine, and went myself with the three remaining men on the pilot engine, both being coupled together. In that way we went slowly along, half the men facing one side of the line, half the other, I myself standing beside the driver of the pilot engine.

MR. CURNOW'S ACCOUNT. 249

In that way we approached Glenrowan station, which was all in darkness. When about fifty yards from the station the driver would insist that there was a man standing on the platform, but it was only his imagination. We pulled up, but not seeing or hearing any one about, we proceeded slowly into the station. I ordered the men to jump on to the platform, and keep a sharp look-out.

In order that the reader may have a clear idea of the events happening at Glenrowan, I break off here my own personal narrative to insert the account given before the police commissioner afterwards, by Mr. Curnow, one of the sixty-two prisoners confined in the hotel by the gang.

"On Sunday morning, 27th June, 1880, I determined to take my wife, sister, and child out for a drive along the road from Glenrowan to Greta. We left the school in a buggy at about eleven o'clock in the morning, accompanied by David Mortimer, my brother-in-law, who rode on horseback. When we got in sight of Mrs. Jones's hotel, and opposite the railway crossing, through which we intended to pass, we noticed a number of people about the hotel, and at the crossing. I said, 'Mrs. Jones must be dead; she has been very ill.' As we got near the hotel, a man ran out of it towards Mrs. Jones's stable, distant about twenty yards from the hotel. I drove past the hotel to the crossing, and, seeing Mr. Stanistreet, asked him, 'What's the matter?' He replied, 'The Kellys are here; you can't go through.' I thought he was joking, and made a motion to drive through the gates, when a man on horseback, who blocked up the crossing, and was talking to a young man whom I knew to be named Delaney, wheeled round his horse and said to me, 'Who are you?' I then saw that he had revolvers in his belt, and was convinced of the truth of Mr. Stanistreet's statement that the Kellys were there. I replied that I was the teacher at Glenrówan. He said, 'Oh! you are the schoolmaster here, are you? and who are those?' pointing to my wife, sister, and brother-in-law. I told him. He then said, 'Where are you going?' I answered, 'Out for a drive.' He then said, 'I am sorry, but I must detain you,' and directed us to get out of the buggy, which we did. He then turned again to Delaney and resumed his conversation with him. I afterwards found that the man who had addressed me was Ned Kelly, the outlaw. I noticed another armed man near Ned Kelly, and I afterwards found out that he was Byrne.

"When we got out of the buggy, I led the horse off the crossing, and tied him to the railway fence alongside, directing Mrs. and Miss Curnow to go into Mr. Stanistreet's house, which they did. As soon as I had fastened the horse, I joined Mr. and Mrs. Stanistreet and others, who I was told had been taken prisoners by the gang, and was informed by them that Glenrowan had been stuck up since three o'clock that morning, and that the gang had forced Reardon and others to tear up part of the railway line beyond the station, for the purpose of wrecking a special train of police and black trackers, which the outlaws said would pass through Glenrowan. Some person—I believe it was one of the boys who had been bailed up by the gang—then told me that the Kellys had been at Beechworth during the previous night, and had shot several policemen.

"After some further conversation, we all listened to what Ned Kelly was saying to Delaney. The outlaw was accusing Delaney of having, some short time previously, ridden a horse from near Greta into Wangaratta to oblige a policeman, and of having sought admission into the police force. He threatened to shoot Delaney for this, and pointed a revolver at him several times. Ned Kelly declared to all of us who were listening to him, that he would have the life of any one who aided the police in any way, or who even showed a friendly feeling for them, and declared that he could and would find them out. He said that a law was made rendering it a crime for any one to help them (the outlaws), and that he would make it a crime for any one to aid the police against the Kelly gang. The women, who were listening to what Kelly was saying, asked him to let Delaney off. After keeping Delaney in a state of extreme terror for about half an hour, the outlaw made him promise never again to seek admission into the police force, and finally said, 'I forgive you this time; but, mind you, be careful for the future.' Byrne then produced a bottle of brandy, and offered some in a tumbler to all adults there. Some accepted it. Byrne drank some himself, and gave Delaney two-thirds of a tumbler, which he drank. Ned Kelly refused to take any, and directed some of his boy prisoners to take my horse and buggy into Mrs. Jones's yard, which they did.

"Ned Kelly and Byrne then went from the railway crossing to Mrs. Jones's hotel, preceded by the majority of their male prisoners, and I was with them. When we reached Mrs. Jones's there were, including those who had just been taken over, about fifty persons in and about the hotel, all of whom appeared to be prisoners of the gang. We were allowed to go about in the hotel, except into one room, which the outlaws used, and of which they kept the key, and we were allowed outside, but were forbidden to leave the premises. Dan Kelly, a short time after I entered the hotel, asked me to have a drink, and I drank with him at the bar. I said to him that I had been told they had been at Beechworth during the previous night, and had shot several police. I asked him whether it was true. He replied that they had been near Beechworth last night, and had done 'some shooting,' and that they had burned the 'devils out,' alluding to police. Byrne came in the bar, and, looking at Dan Kelly's glass, said, 'Be careful, old man.' Dan Kelly replied, 'All right,' and poured water into his brandy. While talking with Byrne and Dan Kelly, I expressed surprise at Glenrowan being stuck up by them, and they said that they had come to Glenrowan in order to wreck a special train of inspectors, police, and black trackers, which would pass through Glenrowan for Beechworth, to take up their trail from there. They said that they had ridden hard across country, often being up to the saddle-girths in water, to get to Glenrowan, and that they had had the line torn up at a dangerous part, and were going to send the train and its occupants to h—l.

"About one o'clock I was standing in the yard of Jones's hotel, thinking of the intentions of the gang, and I keenly felt that it was my duty to do anything that I could to prevent the outrage, which the outlaws had planned, from being accomplished, and I determined that I would try to do so. While standing in the yard, Dan Kelly came out of the hotel and asked me to go inside and have a dance. I said that I could not dance in the boots which I had on. Ned Kelly then came out of the hotel, and hearing me object to dance because of my boots, said, 'Come on; never mind your boots.' I said to him that it was awkward to me to dance in those boots, as I was lame, but that I would dance with pleasure if he would go to the school with me to get a pair of dancing boots. It flashed across my mind that, in passing the Glenrowan police barracks to reach my house, Bracken, the trooper stationed there, might see us, and would be able to give an alarm. I knew that Bracken had been stationed at Greta, and felt sure that he would recognize Ned Kelly. He (Ned Kelly) said that he would go, and we were getting ready, when Dan Kelly interfered, and said that Ned had better stay behind, and let him or Byrne go with me. Some one else also urged Ned Kelly not to go away, and said that my house was near the police barracks. Ned Kelly turned to me, and asked if it was. I said, 'Yes, we shall have to pass the barracks. I had forgotten that.' He then said that he would not go, and I went into the hotel, and danced with Dan Kelly.

"After we had finished dancing, Ned Kelly said that he would go down to the police barracks and bring Bracken, and Reynolds, the postmaster, up to Jones's. I laughed and said to him that I would rather he did it than I, and asked to be allowed to accompany him when he went, and to take home my wife, sister, and child. He gave me no reply. The intention to do something to baffle the murderous designs of the gang grew on me, and I resolved to do my utmost to gain the confidence of the outlaws, and to make them believe me to be a sympathizer with them. I saw clearly that unless I succeeded in doing this, I should not be able to get their permission to go home with my wife, child, and sister, and consequently should not be able to do anything to prevent the destruction of the special train and its occupants, by giving information to the police in Benalla, which I purposed doing if I could induce the outlaws to allow me and mine to go home. The outlaws kept a very sharp watch on their prisoners without seeming to do so.

"About three o'clock in the afternoon Ned and

Dan Kelly caused several of their prisoners to engage in jumping, and in the hop, step, and jump. Ned Kelly joined with them, and used a revolver in each hand as weights. After the jumping was concluded, I left Jones's and went to Mrs. Stanistreet's house to see my wife and sister. They came out to meet me, and noticing the red llama scarf wrapped round my sister caused me to think, 'What a splendid danger signal that would make.' The idea of stopping the train by means of it then entered my mind, and made me still more anxious for liberty. I went with my wife and sister into Mr. Stanistreet's house, and saw Hart lying down on a sofa. He had three loaded guns by his side. He complained to me of having swollen and painful feet, caused, he said, by not having had his boots off for several days and nights. I advised him to bathe them in hot water, and asked for some for him. It was brought, and he followed my advice.

"Shortly after, Mr. Stanistreet and I were walking about at the back of his house, and Mr. Stanistreet expressed a wish that an alarm could be given. Mrs. Stanistreet came out to us, and I asked them if they thought it would be wrong to break a promise given to the outlaws. They said it would not.

I then asked Mr. Stanistreet if the outlaws had taken his revolver from him. He said they had not. I saw what use this fact could be made of by me in my efforts to gain the confidence of the outlaws, and to make them believe that they could safely allow me to go home. I said to Mr. and Mrs. Stanistreet that we had better go inside, for I was afraid of being suspected by the gang if they saw us in private conversation, and we did so. I do not know whether Mr. and Mrs. Stanistreet suspected the use I intended making of my liberty if I got it; but afterwards I heard Mrs. Stanistreet saying to Ned Kelly that he ought to allow me to take home my sister, who was in delicate health.

"I was sitting in Mr. Stanistreet's when Dan Kelly came in, inquiring for a parcel in a small bag, which he had lost. He seemed very anxious about it, and examined the house throughout in search of it. He could not find it, and went to McDonald's hotel to see if it was there. He came back unsuccessful, and I went to Jones's with him, and he searched there, but failed to find it. When he gave up searching for it, I requested him to tell Ned that I wanted to speak to him. I was near the door of Jones's kitchen then. He went

S

into the hotel and brought Ned Kelly out, and I told him that Mr. Stanistreet possessed a loaded revolver from the railway department, and advised them for their safety to obtain it, as some one might get it and do them an injury. They thanked me, and I perceived that I had in a great measure obtained their confidence by telling them this.

"About dusk I heard Ned Kelly saying to Mrs. Jones (they were standing between the hotel and the kitchen, which was a detached building) that he was going down soon to the police barracks to capture Bracken, and that he was going to take her daughter down to call him out. Mrs. Jones asked him not to take her. Ned Kelly said that he did not intend to shoot Bracken, and that her daughter must go. I advanced to them, and said to Ned Kelly that I thought it would be better for him to take Dave Mortimer, my brother-in-law, to call Bracken out, because Bracken knew his voice well, and by hearing it would suspect nothing. Ned Kelly, after a pause, said that he would do so. He then went to Mrs. Jones's stable, and I followed him, and asked if he would allow me to take my party home when he went down for Bracken; and I assured him that he had no cause for fearing me, as I was with him heart and soul.

He replied, 'I know that, and can see it,' and he acceded to my request. I went over to Mrs. Stanistreet's and brought my wife and sister to Mrs. Jones's, and took them into the kitchen. Ned Kelly said that we must wait till he was ready to go. I found, on going back to Jones's, that a log fire had been made on the Wangaratta side of the hotel yard, and that many of the prisoners of the gang were standing around it.

"It was then dark. Other prisoners were in the hotel, and the outlaws encouraged them to amuse themselves by playing cards. I waited with my wife and sister in Jones's kitchen for, I believe, two or three hours, before Ned Kelly directed me to put my horse into the buggy. He and Byrne then went into the room which they had reserved for their own use. I drove to the front of Jones's hotel, and put my wife and sister and Alec Reynolds, the son of the postmaster at Glenrowan, who was about seven years of age, into the buggy. Ned Kelly directed me to take the little boy with us. We were kept waiting in front of the hotel about an hour. Ned Kelly then came to us on horseback, and told me to drive on.

"It was then, I believe, about ten o'clock. As we got into the road, I found that we were accompanied by Ned Kelly, Byrne, and my brother-in-law, each on horseback, and by a Mr. E. Reynolds and R. Gibbins on foot, both of whom resided with Mr. Reynolds, the Glenrowan postmaster. On the road down, Ned Kelly said that he was going to fill the ruts around with the fat carcases of the police. The outlaws each had a light-coloured over-coat on, and I was amazed at the bulky appearance which they presented. I had then no knowledge that the outlaws possessed iron armour. Each one carried a bundle in front of him, and in one hand a gun or a rifle.

"We reached the barracks, and were directed by Ned Kelly to halt about twenty yards distant from the front door of the building. Ned Kelly got off his horse, and fastened him to a fence near, ordering my brother-in-law to do the same, and he did so. Kelly then ordered him to advance to the barracks' door and knock, which he did. Ned Kelly got behind an angle of the walls, and levelled his rifle either at Dave Mortimer, or at the door. No reply came to the knocking or calling, though they were often and loudly repeated at Ned Kelly's whispered command. When I saw Kelly level his rifle, I told my party to get out of the buggy, which they did, and I advanced to my horse's head, for I thought Kelly might fire. I was then about seven or eight yards from Kelly. No result being produced by either knocking or calling, Ned Kelly left his position and advanced to Byrne, directing me, in an undertone, to call Mortimer away, which I did, and he came. Byrne, who had remained near us, and Ned Kelly, then spoke to one another, and Kelly took Alec Reynolds, the postmaster's son, and Mr. E. Reynolds, and passed with them into Reynolds's yard.

"We neither saw nor heard anything for, I think, more than an hour, when Ned Kelly appeared, having Bracken, E. Reynolds, and Bracken's horse with him. Kelly stopped when he reached us, and ordered Bracken to mount the horse brought round, and Bracken did so. Ned Kelly put a halter on the horse, which he kept hold of, saying, 'I can't trust you with the bridle, Bracken.' Bracken said to Ned Kelly that had he not been ill in bed all day he (Kelly) would not have taken him easily, and that if the horse he was on was what it used to be, it would take more than Ned Kelly to keep him a prisoner. Ned Kelly and Byrne mounted their horses, and I and my party got into the buggy.

"It was then, I believe, between eleven and twelve

o'clock. Ned Kelly then said I could go home and take my party with me. He directed us to 'go quietly to bed, and not to dream too loud,' and intimated that if I acted otherwise we would get shot, as one of them would be down at our place during the night to see that we were all right. I then left them and drove home, distant from the barracks one or two hundred yards, leaving the outlaws and their captives ready to start back to the railway station. As soon as we were out of hearing of the outlaws, I announced to my wife and sister my intention to go to Benalla and give information as to the intentions and whereabouts of the outlaws. They both anxiously and earnestly opposed my purpose, saying that it was not at all likely that we should be allowed to come home unless some of the agents of the gang were watching; that I should not be able to reach Benalla, as I should be shot on the road by spies, and that, even if I succeeded, we should be hunted out and shot.

"While the discussion was going on, and supper was being got ready, I quietly prepared everything, including the red llama scarf, candle, and matches, to go to Benalla, intending to keep as close to the railway line as I could, in case of the special coming before I could reach there. I declared to my wife that I did not intend to go by the road—that I meant to keep as close to the line as possible in order to be safer. At last my sister gave way, but my wife worked herself into such an excited and hysterical state, that she declared that she would not leave the house—that if I would go, she would stay there, and she, baby, and my sister would be murdered. I wanted to take them to my mother-in-law's farm, about one-third of a mile from our place, for safety, while I was away. At length Mrs. Curnow consented to go to her mother's to obtain advice, and, as we were momentarily expecting the promised visit from one of the gang, I left the doors unlocked, and wrote a note, leaving it on the table, stating that we were gone to Mrs. Mortimer's to obtain medicine, as Miss Curnow was taken ill. My sister wore her red llama scarf, at my request. When we got there Mrs. Curnow was exceedingly anxious to get home again, and would not stay there, and we went back. I succeeded in persuading Mrs. Curnow to go to bed; and my sister and I told her I had given up my project.

"My sister engaged my wife's attention while I went out to harness my horse to go, for I could not rest, and felt that I must perform what was clearly my duty. I heard the train coming in the distance as I was harnessing the horse, and I immediately caught up the candle, scarf, and matches, and ran down the line to meet the train. I ran on until I got to where I could see straight before me some distance along the line, and where those in the train would be able to see the danger signal. I then lit the candle and held it behind the red scarf.

"As the guard's van got opposite me I caught sight of the guard, who shouted, 'What's the matter?' I yelled, 'The Kellys,' and the pilot engine then stopped a little past me, and the guard jumped down. I told the guard of the line being torn up just beyond the station, and of the Kelly gang lying in wait at the station for the special train of police. He said a special train was behind him, and he would go on to the station and then pull up. I cried, 'No, no! don't you do that, or you will get shot.' He then said that he would go back and stop the special which was coming on. He asked me who I was, and I told him I was the school teacher there, and requested him not to divulge who it was that stopped and warned him, as I was doing it at the risk of my life. He promised to keep my name secret. He asked me to jump in the van, but I declined, as my wife and sister were without protection. The pilot engine whistled several times while I was talking with the guard.

"The pilot went back, and I hastened home, and found Mrs. Curnow had been almost insane while I was stopping the train, and had been made worse by the whistling of the pilot engine. She would not leave the house after I had stopped the train, and we blew out the lights to seem to be in bed. My sister hid the red scarf and my wet clothes, and we were going to deny that it was I who had stopped the train, if one of the outlaws came down to us.

"After the first volleys had been fired, I, with an old man who lived opposite me, went up to Jones's to ascertain who were victorious, but we were ordered back by the police, and we returned home. While I was away my sister and wife had a terrible fright through Mr. Rawlings, who had accompanied the police, coming down to the school. They thought that he was Ned Kelly when he asked for the door to be opened. When I reached home I found Mr. Rawlings there. He asked me to draw a plan of Mrs. Jones's house, which I partly did; but, on hearing the train returning from Benalla, he hurried out, and stopping it, he got into it. During the Sunday afternoon I had heard Mr. Stanistreet ask Ned Kelly to allow the rails torn up to be replaced, and he pointed out to Ned Kelly the sacrifice of innocent lives which would ensue if the Monday morning's passenger train was wrecked. The outlaw refused to allow it to be done. In speaking of and to one another the outlaws had assumed names.

"In the *Argus* report (May 16th) of James Reardon's evidence, given before the Police Commission at Glenrowan, it is stated that James Reardon said he told me that 'the line was broken,' and that he also told me 'how the train could be stopped.' Mr. Reardon is labouring under a wrong impression. I am positive that he did not tell me how the train could be stopped. Stopping the train, nor how to stop it, was not mentioned to me by any one. Of this I am absolutely certain. I have been informed that an impression prevails that it was in my power, before the outlaws stuck up Glenrowan, to have furnished information to the authorities relating to the Kelly gang or their friends. Others assert that I was employed by the authorities to obtain information. I desire to emphatically state that this impression and assertion are both false.

"The outlaws were perfectly sober. One of them, I think Byrne, lay down on the bed about twelve o'clock in the day, and had a sleep, but the others were quite sober."

CHAPTER XI.

The Attack on the Hotel—Wounded.

I MUST now return to my own share in the undertaking. When we arrived at Glenrowan the station was in total darkness. I saw a light in the window of the station-master's house, which was about 100 yards from the platform. I asked a gentleman, Mr. Rawlings, who had come with me from Benalla in our special, to accompany me to the station-master's house, leaving all the men on the platform, telling them to keep a sharp look-out during my absence. I knocked at the window, and a woman, who was crying, opened it. I said to her, "Where is your husband?" She would not answer me. I asked her two or three times and could get no reply. At last I said, "My good woman, do calm yourself and answer me. I will see no harm come to you." She said nothing, but pointed in the direction of the Warby Ranges, and also in the direction of the hotel. I took her to mean that he was taken into the ranges. I said, "Who took him away?" She replied, "The Kellys." I said, "How long ago?" She replied, "Ten minutes."

I must here state that Hart guarded the station-master in his own house, and was with him the greater part of the night, and when he heard my train stop about a mile away he took Stanistreet, the station-master, up to Jones's hotel, and reported the matter to Ned Kelly. Stanistreet was put in with the remainder of the prisoners. Their object in doing this was, that they thought when the special arrived at Glenrowan the train might require some signal before it would pass, and that they would compel the station-master to give this while they covered him with their pistols. I left Mrs. Stanistreet, and returned to the platform with Rawlings. I told my men that the Kellys had been there ten minutes ago and had taken away the station-master, and ordered our horses to be taken out of the train as quickly as possible.

I had hardly given these orders, when I heard the sentry placed at the back of the platform call out, "Who goes there?" The reply was "Police." I saw a man getting over the back of the platform, and heard him calling out my name. I said, "Who is it?" He replied, "Bracken. Go quickly over to Mrs. Jones's,

THE BEGINNING OF THE ATTACK. 269

the outlaws are all there, and if you don't go this moment they will be gone." I called on the men to follow me. A voice cried out, "What shall I do with the horses?" I said, "Let them go." The men, when taking out the horses, had put down their arms and ammunition on the platform, and in the hurry had a difficulty in finding them. I called out, "Come on, men, or they will be gone." I saw two men standing beside me ready to start, and off I hurried, accompanied by these two. By the path we took, the hotel would be about 200 yards from the platform. I looked round whilst running, and saw several of the men following me.

The hotel, which was in total darkness, was a weather-board house with a verandah in front; not a sound came from it. The moon was setting behind the house; our approach could be seen distinctly by any one standing under the verandah, which to us was in total darkness. When I was within sixteen yards of the verandah I saw a flash, and heard a report from a rifle, fired from about a yard in front of the verandah, and my left hand dropped beside me. Three flashes came from under the verandah. The man who fired the first shot stepped back under the verandah, and began firing upon us. He called out, "Fire away, you beggars, you can do us no harm." One of the men beside me said, "That is Ned Kelly's voice." The four outlaws continued firing some minutes; I suppose they must have fired thirty or forty shots at us, as they had repeating rifles and revolvers. My men returned the fire very briskly; I fancy we must have fired at least fifty or sixty shots, for there were not only my men, but the trackers also, who were blazing away as hard as they could fire. We could only fire in the direction from which the flashes came, as the figures of the men were invisible in the darkness.

When we commenced firing, we were unaware there was any one in the house, until we heard the most fearful shrieks coming from inside the hotel from men, women, and children. We discovered afterwards that the front of the building, which the outlaws were standing against, was composed of thin weather-boards, and the Martini-Henry bullets were going through the building amongst the occupants. Two or three children were shot. There was a general cry to lie down, Bracken, with great forethought, before he left the house, having told them to do so. By this means most of them escaped without injury. Eventually the outlaws retreated inside the hotel, which was still in total darkness. There must have been a terrible scene inside.

NIGHT ATTACK ON THE GLENROWAN HOTEL.

WOUNDED.

The moment the outlaws retreated into the house I ordered my men to cease firing, and told them to surround the hotel and see that no one escaped, whilst I went to the railway platform to have my arm bandaged. It was bleeding fearfully; a bullet had entered one side of my wrist and gone out at the other. I went to the platform, where I found some of the reporters, one of whom kindly bandaged my wrist up. I made arrangements for a train to be sent to Benalla to inform the officer in charge of what had occurred, and to send a few more men up, as I had no notion what effect the firing had taken upon the outlaws.

At this time I had no idea how serious my wound was, as I had not felt very much pain in it. I then returned to the hotel. I tried to get through the fence, but was unable either to get over it or through it, in consequence of my hand being useless. I could see that the men had taken up their positions surrounding the house, and sat down in a position where I also had good command over the house. Having remained there about a quarter of an hour I began to feel very faint and dizzy; the wound was bleeding copiously. I attempted to stand up, but had great difficulty in doing so. I managed, however, to get back to the platform, but fell down in a faint from loss of blood. Some restoratives were given me and I recovered consciousness. I was put on the second engine that was at the platform, and sent to Benalla, the blood still running fast from the wound. On my arrival there it was five o'clock. I found a gentleman on the platform, and I asked him to accompany me to the doctor's house, and then to the telegraph station. Before I left Glenrowan I told them all I would be back immediately. I called at the doctor's, told him I had been wounded by Kelly, and requested him to follow me to the telegraph station, as I wanted to communicate with the other stations, and get them to send some assistance.

When I got to the telegraph office I was much exhausted, and terribly excited. I could not write, but got the telegraph master to write to my dictation. I sent messages to all surrounding stations, and just as I had finished, the doctor came in. He took the handkerchief off my arm and said that I was bleeding from the artery. I asked him to attend to it at once, as I wished to return to Glenrowan. The officer in charge also came into the office and I said, "Don't go without me, I shall be all right in a few minutes." His answer was, "Don't be such a glutton, you have got one bullet in you, and you want more." I said I was determined to go back. I remember their pulling a mattress on to the floor of the telegraph office, and my lying on it, and then I fainted away and continued unconscious for some time. When I recovered consciousness I felt terribly weak, and could scarcely stand. I was assisted to my hotel and went to bed.

I have hitherto merely given my personal experiences with reference to the capture of the Kelly gang, but I think the history would hardly be complete without a full account of all that transpired at Glenrowan during the capture. I have, therefore, taken the following narrative from *The Age* newspaper of the 29th of June, 1880—they had their own correspondent on the ground during the fight. A few errors have crept in, and these I have corrected in brackets; but on the whole it is a very fair account of what took place.

CHAPTER XII.

From *The Age* Newspaper, 29th June, 1880—The Start—The Journey—A Timely Warning—The Gang surprised—Death of Byrne—Capture of Ned Kelly—His Statement—The Prisoners released—Renewal of the Fight.

BENALLA, *Monday Night.*

IMMEDIATELY on the receipt of the news by Captain Standish on Sunday night that the Kellys had at last broken cover, and committed another diabolical outrage near Beechworth, he ordered a special train at once to start from Spencer Street. He was induced to do so because of the fact that Sub-inspector O'Connor had, with his black trackers, been withdrawn from the Kelly country. They were on the eve of their departure for Queensland, and were staying at Essendon. Captain Standish ordered the special train to convey the blacks to the scene of the outrage, so that they might there pick up the tracks of the dreaded gang; but no one at that time imagined that the expedition would have such a speedy and sensational termination; that, in fact, it would end in the annihilation of the band in a manner that must strike terror into the hearts of all sympathizers and men inclined to imitate the doings of the gang. When the news arrived at the station that a special train was required, all the engines were cold, and it was not till a quarter past ten o'clock that a start was made; and the small party of press gentlemen, who in good spirits took their seats in the carriage, little thought that the journey they were undertaking was of such a perilous nature. Only one gentleman was armed. At Essendon Inspector O'Connor and his five black trackers were picked up, together with Mrs. O'Connor and her sister, Miss Smith. [Those ladies intended to proceed to Beechworth and remain there whilst we went in pursuit of the gang.] The men were evidently in excellent spirits at the prospect of an encounter. The train proceeded rapidly on its way. At Craigieburn it ran through a gate, which carried away the brake of the engine, and necessitated a stoppage of about twenty minutes. After that, fair progress was made to Benalla, where Superintendent Hare, who was in waiting with eight men and seventeen horses, joined the party. Mr. Chas. C. Rawlings also became one of the number. The night was a splendid one, the moon shining with unusual brightness, whilst the sharp frosty air caused the slightest noise in the forest beyond to be distinctly heard. It was thought that the Kellys or some of their friends might place an obstruction on the line, and in order that danger in this direction should be avoided as much as possible, it was determined to lash one of the police to the front of the engine, so that he might there keep a good look-out. At the last moment this plan was abandoned, and it is a merciful intervention of Providence that it was so. Time certainly was lost by the change of tactics, but the loss was gain. There was a spare engine in the station, and it was determined to use this as a pilot. [The pilot was arranged for early in the afternoon.] Accordingly, it started about half a mile ahead of the special [only 100 yards], which it was intended to run through to Beechworth. Glenrowan is the next station to Benalla, being about fourteen miles distant.

However, when within a mile and a quarter of Glenrowan, just opposite Playford's and De Soir's paddocks, the special came to a sudden halt. Danger signals from the pilot engine were the cause, and in a very few seconds the pilot came back with an intimation that a man, in a state of great excitement, had stopped the engine, and had stated that Glenrowan was stuck up by the Kellys, who had torn up the lines just beyond the station in order to destroy the party which they knew would pass along the line in the special. The news and the stated intentions of the gang had not a cheering effect, but the police displayed an eagerness for action. The members of the press barricaded their windows with the cushions upon which they had previously sat, and in response to the request which some of the number made, the lights in the train were extinguished. It was then ten minutes to three o'clock, and Superintendent Hare was not long in determining what to do. The man who gave the information disappeared in the forest as soon as he had imparted his news, and his story was accepted with caution; but it was soon made apparent that he had saved the lives of those in the train, which to a certainty would, along with the pilot engine, have been hurled into a deep gully just below the Glenrowan Station, and behind a curve in the line which would have prevented the conductors from seeing the pilot go over the embankment where the rails had been torn up. Mr. Hare, with one or two of the police, proceeded in the pilot engine to the railway station, closely followed by the special. On arriving at the station the horses were quickly got out of the trucks by the men, whilst Mr. Hare, with one or two men and Mr. Rawlings, proceeded towards the Glenrowan Hotel to seek information. Mr. Rawlings, when he left Benalla, jocularly made a boast that they would bring back the remains of the outlaws. He little thought at that time that his prediction would prove to be absolutely correct.

The township of Glenrowan consists of about half a dozen houses, inclusive of two bush hotels, Jones's Glenrowan Hotel being about 200 yards from the station, on the west side of the line, whilst M'Donald's Hotel is about the same distance on the other side of the line. In an instant the men on the platform were convinced, by the report of a shot fired from Jones's Hotel, that they were in the presence of the desperate outlaws. [This is an error; no shot was fired until we were within sixteen yards of the hotel.] The next few minutes were productive of painful excitement. The police abandoned the horses and rushed to their arms. The black trackers sprang forward with their leader, and soon took up a good position in front of the house. Mr. Hare could be plainly seen by the light of the moon. He walked towards the hotel, and when within about twenty-five yards of the verandah, the tall figure of a man came round the corner, and fired. The shot took effect on Mr. Hare's wrist. Senior-constable Kelly and Rawlings were close to him, and the former promptly returned the fire, which was taken up by Hare, although wounded, and Mr. Rawlings followed his example.

Just before Superintendent Hare was wounded, Constable Bracken, the local policeman, who had been made prisoner in the hotel, courageously made his escape, and running towards the railway station, quickly spread the information that the Kellys, with about forty prisoners, were inmates of the hotel, which was a weather-board building, containing about six rooms, inclusive of the bar. Behind the building there was a kitchen, the walls of which were constructed of slabs. Into this the police fired. When about sixty shots had been sent into the walls of the building, the clear voice of Hare was distinguished above the screams of the terrified women and children who were in the hotel, giving the order to stop firing. This was now repeated by Senior-constable Kelly to the men who, under cover, were surrounding the house at the back, but the Kellys fired three or four more shots, after which one of them gave vent to coarse and brutal language, calling to the police, "Come on, you —— wretches, and you can fire away; you can never harm us." A few straggling shots were then fired, the sharp sounds of the rifle being echoed from the mount called Morgan's Lookout, at the foot of which the fight took place.

Then all was silent again, and after the lapse of about a quarter of an hour Superintendent Hare approached the station and stated that he had been wounded in the wrist. The wound was a very bad one, and was bleeding very much. There was no doctor present, but the representatives of the press succeeded in stopping the rapid loss of blood. During the trying ordeal, Mrs. O'Connor and Miss Smith remained unwilling witnesses of the terrible scene. They retained their seats in the railway carriage, and the courage which they displayed, notwithstanding that the bullets from the outlaws whistled past the train, surely ought to have had a good effect on the men who were facing death in the execution of their duty. Seeing the wound, the ladies implored Mr. Hare not to return to the fight, but he did so. His re-appearance in the trenches was the signal for renewed firing, and the valley was soon filled with smoke. Mr. Hare then became faint from loss of blood, and was compelled to leave the field. He went back to Benalla on an engine in order to have his injury attended to, and to send more men to the front.

A long and tedious interval followed, during which time Mr. Stanistreet, the station-master, suddenly left the hotel, where he had been kept prisoner with the other residents of Glenrowan. He walked boldly away, and had a narrow escape of being shot by the police, but he saved himself by proclaiming he was the station-master. He reported that the gang were still in the house, and that the shots of the police had struck the daughter of Mrs. Jones, a girl fourteen years of age, on the head, whilst the son, John Jones, a boy of nine years, was wounded in the hip. Very soon after this, painful, hysterical screams of terror were heard from Mrs. Jones and a Mrs. Reardon, both of whom were walking about the place, disregarding the danger to be feared from the volleys which the police, at short intervals, poured into the hotel. Mrs. Jones's grief occasionally took the form of vindictiveness towards the police, whom she called murderers. The police frequently called upon the women to come away, but they hesitated, and Mrs. Reardon and her son were afraid to accompany Mr. Reardon to the station. The poor woman was carrying a baby only a few months old in her arms, and she eventually ran to the station, where she received every kindness from the persons there assembled. She was then in a very terrified condition, and told the following story, which serves to show the manner in which the gang took possession of Glenrowan.

She said: " My husband is a plate-layer, employed on the railway, and we live about a mile from the station, on the Benalla side. At three o'clock on Sunday morning we were all in bed. We were aroused by Ned Kelly, who knocked at the door, and told my husband, when he opened it, to surrender. He advised us to dress, and I did so. They had also made a prisoner of Sullivan, another plate-layer, and Kelly brought us to the station, where I was kept for some hours. Kelly took my husband and Sullivan down the line, in order to tear up the line and destroy the train with the police. He was afterwards taken to the hotel. There are a lot of innocent people in there now, and they are frightened to come out for fear the police will kill them. Amongst the people who are in there are:— James and Michael Reardon, my husband and son, Catherine and William Rennison, John and Patrick Delaney (who are here coursing), W. S. Cooke (a labourer), Martin Sherry (a plate-layer), John Larkins

ARRIVAL OF MORE POLICE.

(a farmer), Edward Reynolds (the brother of the postmaster), Robert Gibbons, the brothers Meanliffe, and other strangers I do not know."

When the poor woman had completed her story, the firing of the police became very brisk, and it was replied to by the desperadoes in the hotel. Senior-constable Kelly at that juncture found a rifle stained with blood lying on the side of the hill, and this led to the supposition that one of the gang had been wounded, and had escaped through the forest towards Morgan's Look-out. Just then nine police with Superintendent Sadleir and Dr. Hutchinson came from Benalla. Almost immediately after, seven policemen under Sergeant Steele arrived on horseback from Wangaratta. The alarm had been given there by Trooper Bracken, who caught a horse and rode the ten miles in a surprisingly short space of time. The conduct of Bracken, and the promptitude of the Wangaratta police, is to be highly commended. Just before their arrival a heavy volley was poured into the hotel by the police.

According to the statement of some of the prisoners, afterwards made, that volley proved fatal to Joe Byrne, who was standing close to young Delaney, drinking a nobbler of whisky at the bar, when he was shot in the groin. He was then carried to the back of the building, where he gradually sank and died a painful death. This fact at the time was unknown to the police.

The morning broke beautiful and clear. The police were disposed all round the hotel, when they were beset by a danger from the rear. Ned Kelly was the cause. It appears he was the man who shot Mr. Hare, and he himself was wounded in the arm by the fire which was returned. He could not without danger get into the hotel, so he sprang upon his horse, and during the excitement which followed, he got away towards Morgan's Look-out, but it was not the intention of the bold ruffian to desert his comrades, and he returned to fight his way to them. [This is quite wrong. Kelly being wounded, tried to escape on foot, but being shot in the foot was unable to walk. No man left the hotel on horseback, but, to make a hero of himself, he told this story.]

It was nearly eight o'clock when his tall figure was seen close behind the line of police. At first it was thought he was a black fellow. He carried a grey coat over his arm, [he wore the coat over his armour], and walked coolly and slowly among the police. His head, chest, back, and sides were all pro-

NED KELLY IN HIS ARMOUR.

tected with heavy plates of quarter-inch iron. When within easy distance of Senior-constable Kelly, who was watching him, he fired. The police then knew who he was, and Sergeant Steele, Senior-constable Kelly, with Mr. Dowsett (a railway guard), fired on the ruffian. The contest became one which, from its remarkable nature, almost baffles description. Nine police joined in the conflict and fired point blank at Kelly; but although, in consequence of the way in which he staggered, it was apparent that many of the shots hit him, yet he always recovered himself, and tapping his breast, laughed derisively at his opponents, as he coolly returned the fire, fighting only with a revolver. It appeared as if he was a fiend with a charmed life.

For half an hour this strange contest was carried on, and then Sergeant Steele rapidly closed in on him, and when within only about ten yards of him, fired two shots into his legs which brought the outlaw down. He was only wounded, and appeared still determined to carry on the desperate conflict, but Steele bravely rushed him and seized the hand in which he held his revolver, the only weapon with which he was armed. He fired one shot after this, but without effect. When on the ground he roared with savage ferocity, cursing the police vehemently. He was stripped of his armour, and then became quite submissive, and was borne to the railway station by Sergeant Steele, Constable Dwyer, and two representatives of the Melbourne press.

Great praise is due to Guard Dowsett for the plucky manner in which he assisted the police. He was armed with a revolver, and got very close to the outlaw. At the railway station Kelly appeared to be very weak from the loss of blood, and some brandy was given him. He was examined in the guard's van by Dr. Nicholson and Dr. Hutchinson, who found that he was suffering from two bullet wounds in the left arm, a bullet in the right foot near the right toe, and two wounds in the right leg, those inflicted by Sergeant Steele.

The outlaw was quite composed, and in answer to inquiries he made the following statement :—" What I intended to do, and in fact was just about doing, was to go down with some of my mates and meet the special train and rake it with shot. The train, however, came before I expected, and I had to return to the hotel. I thought the train would go on, and on that account I had the rails pulled up, so that these —— black trackers might be settled. It does not much matter what brought me to Glenrowan. I do not know, or I do not say. It does not seem much, any way. If I liked, I could have got away last night. I got into the bush with my grey mare, and laid there all night. I had a good chance, but I wanted to see the thing end.

"When the police fired the first round I got wounded in the foot. It was the left one. Shortly afterwards I was shot through the left arm. It was in the front of the house where I received these injuries. I don't care what people say about Sergeant Kennedy's death. I have made my statement as to it, and if they don't believe me I can't help it. At all events, I am satisfied Scanlan was not shot kneeling. That is not true. He never got off his horse. At the commencement of the affair this morning I fired three or four shots from the front of Jones's Hotel, but I do not know who I was firing at. I only fired when I saw flashes. I then cleared for the bush, but remained there near the hotel all night. Two constables passed close by me talking, and I could have shot them before I had time to shout, if I liked. I could have shot several constables at one time. I was a good distance away, but I came back again. I have got a charge of duck-shot in my leg. Why don't the police use bullets instead of duck-shot?

"One of the policemen that was firing at me was

a splendid shot. I don't know his name. Perhaps I would have done better if I had cleared away on my grey mare. [He never had a chance.] It was just like blows from a man's fist receiving the bullets on my armour. I wanted to fire into the carriages, only the police started on us too quickly. I knew the police would come, and I expected them."

Inspector Sadleir here remarked, "You wanted then to kill the people in the train?" Kelly replied, "Yes; of course I did. God help them, they would have got shot all the same. Would they not have tried to kill me?" Every kindness was shown to Kelly by the police, and his two sisters were permitted to remain with him during the afternoon. He was also seen by Father Tierney, to whom it is understood he made a confession, but the reverend gentleman courteously declined to state the nature of it.

At various times during the morning more police arrived, but the bushrangers could not be dislodged; and what was more perplexing still, the prisoners inside could not be persuaded to leave, although the police repeatedly called upon them to come out. At twelve o'clock, however, the people inside, consisting of about thirty men and youths, suddenly rushed out of the front door, carrying their hands aloft. The police told them to advance towards where they were located, but many of the unfortunate people were so terror-stricken that they ran hither and thither screaming for mercy. They then approached the police and threw themselves upon their faces.

One by one they were called on, and having been minutely searched, were despatched to the station. When the turn of two youths named M'Auliffe came, Superintendent Sadleir directed Constable Bracken to arrest them as Kelly sympathizers. They were accordingly handcuffed, and taken with the others to the railway-station. Young Reardon, who with his father had been confined in the hotel, was severely wounded in the shoulder by a bullet fired from a rifle in the hands of one of the police. The unfortunate youth was at once attended to by the doctors already named. Although the wound was a serious one, it was not considered such as would prove fatal.

The police after this kept up a constant fire on the place, Dwyer and Armstrong in front of the house, Andrew Clarke, sen., and Constable Kelly getting very close in at various quarters of attack. It was noticed that the fire from the besieged bushrangers was not returned after one o'clock, but it was believed that Dan Kelly and Hart intended to lie quiet until night, and under cover of the darkness make their escape. The police for a time also ceased firing. A consultation was held amongst the officers as to what was to be done next. During the cessation of hostilities I visited the locality where the line had been torn up; it is about three-quarters of a mile on the Wangaratta side of Glenrowan. Several lengths of rails had been wrenched from their places at a curve terminating at a rapid decline, and had not timely warning been given, the pilot-engine, followed closely by the special, would have inevitably toppled over an embankment into a defile over thirty feet in depth. I arrived back at the station in time to witness the most tragic and exciting scene of the day. The police had telegraphed for a field-gun from Melbourne, but fearing it would not arrive in time to be of any use, it was determined to adopt another mode of dislodging the remaining outlaws.

CHAPTER XIII.

From *The Age* (continued). Mrs. Skillian comes on the Scene —The Hotel fired—Rescue of Sherry—Fate of Dan Kelly and Hart—Statement of Various Prisoners made by the Gang—The Incident of the Cannon.

JUST as they were about to put this newly-conceived plan into operation, Mrs. Skillian, sister of the Kellys, dressed in a dark riding-habit trimmed with scarlet, and wearing a jaunty hat adorned with a conspicuous white feather, appeared on the scene. Father Tierney earnestly requested her to go to the hotel and ask her brother and Hart to surrender. She said she would like to see her brother before he died, but she would sooner see him burned in the house than ask him to surrender. This, in fact, was the procedure which the police had decided upon in order to bring the outlaws from their cover. Some 200 people by this time had arrived on the platform.

The police opened up a heavy fire on the hotel from the front and rear. This was done in order to cover the operations of Senior-constable John stone, who rapidly approached the house on the north side with a bundle of straw, which he placed against the weather-boards and set fire to. It was known that Martin Sherry, an old man, was still in the house, and when the last prisoners had escaped he was alive, though badly wounded. The thought that the unfortunate man would be sacrificed, and perish in the flames with the determined bushrangers who had made so long a stand, caused a feeling of horror to pervade the crowd.

Kate Kelly at this juncture came upon the scene, but the only expression which escaped her lips was the one uttered in heart-broken accents, " My poor, poor brother." Mrs. Skillian exclaimed, " I will see my brother before he dies," and then sped towards the hotel, from the roof of which by this time tongues of flame were beginning to ascend. The police ordered her to go back, and she hesitated.

Father Tierney emerged from the crowd, saying he would save Sherry. The brave clergyman was encouraged on his mission by a cheer from the spectators. He walked boldly to the front door, was lost to view amongst the smoke, and directly afterwards a mass of flames burst from the walls and roof of the dwelling at the same instant. A shout of terror from the crowd announced the fear that was felt for the safety of the courageous priest. Constable Armstrong, with some other policemen, rushed into the building from the rear, and a few seconds afterwards their forms, with that of Father Tierney, were seen to emerge, carrying with them Sherry, who was in a dying state, and the dead body of the outlaw Byrne.

On reaching a place of safety they stated that Dan Kelly and Hart were lying upon the floor apparently dead. Nothing, however, could be done to rescue their remains from the fire. Soon afterwards the building was completely demolished, and on a search being made amongst the ruins, two charred skeletons were raked out from the smouldering *débris*. Wild, Wright, Hart (the brother of Steve), and other well-known friends were witnesses of this terrible scene. All the bushrangers were clad in the same kind of armour as that worn by Ned Kelly, which weighed as much as ninety-seven pounds, and had evidently been constructed by some country blacksmith out of ploughshares. The marks on Kelly's armour showed that he had been hit seventeen times with bullets.

The unfortunate man Sherry died soon after being rescued from the burning building. Ned Kelly was brought on to Benalla by the evening train, and lodged in the lock-up, to await the inquest to be held in the morning.

The statement of Constable Bracken is to the effect that the first intimation of the presence of the gang at Glenrowan was on Sunday night at eleven o'clock, when he was bailed up by Ned Kelly. He had been confined to bed through illness. Whilst a prisoner in the hotel he courageously managed to steal the key of the front door, which enabled him to escape in time to warn the police that the outlaws were in the house.

Mr. John Stanistreet, station-master at Glenrowan, states—"About three o'clock on Sunday morning a knock came to my door, at the gatehouse, within one hundred yards of the station, on the Melbourne side. I jumped up, and thinking it was some one wanting to get through the gates in a hurry, I commenced to dress as soon as possible. I half dressed, and went to the door. Just when I got there it was burst in, but previous to that there was some impatient talk, which caused me to dress quickly. When the door was burst in I asked, 'What is that for?' or 'Who are you?' The answer was, 'I am Ned Kelly.' I then saw a man, clad in an overcoat, standing in the doorway. He pushed me into my bedroom, where my wife and some of the children were in bed. There were two girls and one infant besides my wife. Then he said to me, 'You have to come with me and take up the rails.' 'Wait,' said I, 'until I dress.' He said, 'Yes,' and I completed my dressing and followed him out of the house.

"On the line there were seven or eight men standing at the gate which crosses the line to Mrs. Jones's hotel, the Glenrowan Inn. He said, 'You direct those men how to raise some of the rails, as we expect a special train very soon.' I objected, saying, 'I know nothing about lifting rails off the line; the only persons who understand it are the repairers; they live outside and along the line.' Ned Kelly then went into Reardon the plate-layer's house. Reardon lives outside the line on the Greta side about a quarter of a mile away. Steve Hart was present, and Kelly left us in his charge. When Kelly went away Hart gave me a prod with his rifle in the side, saying, 'You get the tools out that are necessary to raise those rails.' I said, 'I have not the key of the chest;' and he said, 'Break the lock.' He told one of the men to do so, and on arriving at the station he got one of the men to do it. This was in the little back shed used as a store-room, between the station and the gatehouse. The tools were thrown out, and in the meantime Reardon and Sullivan, the line-repairers, arrived with Ned Kelly. These two men and Ned proceeded down the line towards Wangaratta to lift the rails. We were still under Steve Hart, and we remained where we were over two hours, and then Ned Kelly and the repairers returned. Ned then inquired about the signalling of trains, as to how I stopped a train with the signal-lights. I said, '"White is right, red is wrong, and green is gently, come along."' He said, 'There is a special train coming; you give no signals.' Speaking to Hart he said, 'Watch his countenance, and if he gives any signal, shoot him.' He then marched us into my residence, and left us there under Steve Hart. There were there then about seventeen altogether, other persons subsequently being placed in my house also. There were present Reardon's family, the Ryan family, Cameron (son of the gatekeeper on the other line), Sullivan, line-repairer, and others whom I do not remember. We were locked up all day on Sunday, and were only allowed out under surveillance. The women were permitted to go to Jones's Hotel about five o'clock, and shortly afterwards all the men but me and my family went away. Steve Hart stopped with us, and during the night Dan Kelly relieved Hart, and he was afterwards relieved by Byrne.

"Just before the special train arrived I was ordered to the hotel by Hart, who was on and off duty all the time, to follow him to Jones's, and not signal the train. I went into the back kitchen, where Mrs. Jones and daughter, aged about fourteen, and two younger children were. There was also a man there named Neil M'Kew. By this time the train had arrived, and firing was going on furiously. I did not see Ned Kelly in the room. I with others stood in the chimney. I did not hear any remark passed by any of the gang, and they disappeared. A ball passed through the hut, and grazed Miss Jane Jones, fourteen years of age, on the forehead. The girl said, 'I'm shot,' and turned to me. I saw the blood and told her it was nothing. The mother commenced to cry, and soon afterwards I left the kitchen, and went into the back-yard. I then saw three of the gang there standing behind the chimney. They had their rifles in their hands. One of them said, I don't know which, 'If you go out you'll be shot.' I walked straight down the path towards the house. The firing was then going on all round me, but I was uninjured. One of the police very nearly shot me, but I said

'Station-master' when he challenged me. I forgot to mention that during Sunday afternoon Steve Hart demanded and received my revolver."

Robert Gibbons states—"I am a farmer, and have recently been stopping at Glenrowan with Mr. Reynolds. I came to the railway-station about eight o'clock on Sunday night with Mr. Reynolds to ask about his little boy, who had not been home. When we knocked at the door, Mrs. Stanistreet told us that Mr. Hart was inside, and that they had been stuck up ever since three o'clock on Sunday morning. We followed her in, and saw Steve Hart. She told him who we were, and he then put his fire-arms down, giving us to understand that we were not to go out. We remained there about two hours, when Ned Kelly came, and Hart ordered us to come out of the room. Ned Kelly then told us that we would all have to go down to the police-barracks with him. He kept us waiting there for about two hours, he having gone for Bracken. He returned to us with Bracken. He kept us waiting there about an hour and a half. Byrne at that time was with us. There he told me and Mr. Reynolds we would have to go to Jones's Hotel. We went to the hotel, and he told us to get into the bar parlour. It was then about ten o'clock on Sunday night, and we remained there until the train came. During that time the Kellys were going about the place making themselves quite jolly. Byrne was in charge of the back-door, the other door being locked. A little after three o'clock the train came. Prior to that the gang drank quite freely with the others. When the train arrived, Ned came and said, 'You are not to whisper a word that has been said here about me. If I hear of any one doing so I will shoot you.' He went to the door of the room and said, 'Here she comes,' and then the gang busied themselves in making preparations, but for what I did not know. They came back and said the first man who left the room in which we were would be shot. Two of them then mounted their horses, and rode away, but I could not tell which two. They came back in about ten minutes' time. When they came back, I saw that Dan was one of the two who had gone away. Dan went into a back room. All four in turn went into the same room. Very soon afterwards a hurried move was made, and firing commenced. There must have been about forty men, women, and children in the house then. The women and children commenced to shriek, and Mrs. Jones's eldest daughter was wounded on the side of the head, and the eldest boy shot in the thigh. The bullets rattled through the side of the house, and we laid down. We were packed so close that we had to lie on our sides. It was those who laid next the door who prompted us to come out, and we did so because we feared that the bullets would come through faster than ever. We also feared a cannon would be used; and about ten o'clock we ran out. I heard some of them say that Bryne, or one of the gang, was lying dead in the back. I know that Dan was alive when I left."

Arthur Loftus Mauld Steele states—"I am a sergeant of police at Wangaratta. I arrived here with five men about five a.m. We were at once challenged by police, and answered, 'Wangaratta police.' My men were then distributed around the hut, and I got to the tree near the back door of the hut. There was no firing then. A woman and child came to the back-door screaming, and I told the woman if she ran in quick she would not be molested. A man then came to the back-door, and I asked him to throw up his arms or I would fire on him. He was only about twenty-five yards distant. The man stooped and ran towards the stables and I fired. He then turned and ran back to the house, and I fired again. I am certain I hit him with the second shot, as he screamed and fell against the door. There was then some hot firing, and the bullets whistled all around me. The firing was kept up for some time, and some of the men behind me called out. It was then breaking day. I looked round, and saw a man stalking down. I thought he was a black-fellow, and called on the others to be careful. I then saw him present a revolver and fire at the police. I could see the bullets hitting him, and staggering him for a moment, with no further effect. I therefore thought he had armour on, and determined to have a close shot at him. I ran towards him, and when within ten yards of him he saw me, and turned round to fire at me. I then aimed at his legs, and he staggered, but he still tried to aim at me. I then fired the second barrel on the legs. We were then in the open. He fell, and cried, 'I'm done, I'm done.' I ran up to him then, and he again tried to shoot me, but I caught the revolver and pushed it down. I was behind him, and he could not turn on me quick enough to shoot me. Whilst I held the revolver away from me he fired the revolver. Senior-constable Kelly then came up and assisted me to secure him. So did O'Dwyer, and a host of others at once followed. We only found one revolver on him, and a bag of ammunition. We divested him of his armour. I was strained after the scuffle which ensued."

Senior-constable Kelly states—"When we started from the platform we ran down towards the railway-gates, hearing that the gang were in Jones's public-house. The men at that time had not sufficient time to scatter, and all made towards the hotel. As we approached, some one came out on the verandah and fired on us. Mr. Superintendent Hare, with Mr. Rawlings, a volunteer from Benalla, was close to me. Mr. Hare said, 'I am shot in the wrist,' but he continued to fire. We sought cover, and Hare said to me, 'For God's sake, surround the house, and don't let them escape.' He then fired again, and gave the gun to Rawlings. He then left, saying, 'Kelly, place the men under cover,' and I placed the men around the house. Mr. O'Connor and his trackers took up a position in front of the hotel. I then went round towards the back of the premises. Constable Arthur was with me, and we crawled about 400 yards. In this way we got to within about fifty yards of the house, at the back of a tree. In the scrub I found a revolving rifle covered with blood, and a padded skull-cap." [This was Ned Kelly's. Being wounded in the thumb, he could not use his rifle.] "We kept strict watch, and fired upon any one who attempted to leave the hut. There were four horses saddled and tied up to the back-door. These we shot in order to prevent the sudden escape of the gang. When we left the station we met Constable Bracken, who told us that the gang were at Jones's. He, I believe, jumped on one of our horses, and rode off to Benalla to get further assistance, and at half-past six o'clock he returned with the Wangaratta police, Sergeant Steele being at their head. We continued to fire, and at about eight o'clock, so far as I can remember, Ned Kelly made his appearance under the brow of the hill, 300 yards from the hut. He deliberately fired at me. I returned the fire, and my men closed around him, Sergeant Steele being behind him, myself on one side, and Dowsett, the railway-guard, on the other. About ten rifles were brought to bear on him, and we hit him several times. His heavy armour, however, protected him, and he walked boldly to and fro. Near a fallen tree he fell, and we rushed forward. I caught him by the head as Steele grasped his hand, in which he still held his revolver. He fired it, but did no damage. His armour was taken off, and he was carried to the railway-station, where he was searched, but only threepence was found on him, a silver Geneva watch, and a lot of ammunition. I asked him to tell me where Sergeant Kennedy's watch was, and he said, 'I cannot tell you; I would not like to tell you about it.' He also said, 'I had to shoot Sergeant Kennedy and Scanlan for my own safety. I cannot tell you any more.' We then gave him over to the medical gentleman and Mr. Sadleir."

During the forenoon Colonel Anderson received information from Captain Standish that in order to dislodge the two remaining members of the gang without endangering any further life, the hotel would have to be blown down, and as the best means for accomplishing that object, a small cannon would probably be required. The Commandant, telegraphing for further particulars in order to guide him in the selection of a gun, received from Superintendent Sadleir the following reply—"Glenrowan.—Weatherboard, brick chimneys, slab kitchen. The difficulty we feel is that our shots have no effect on the corner, and there are so many windows that we should be under fire all the day. We must get the gun before night, or rush the place." Immediately upon the receipt of this message, Colonel Anderson arranged for the supply of a twelve-pound Armstrong gun, which was quickly placed upon a truck at the Spencer-street station. A special train was soon in readiness, and at twenty minutes past two it departed, carrying the formidable-looking weapon, a detachment of the Garrison Artillery under Lieutenant Nicholson, and the Commandant himself. The train, in order to land the gun at the scene of action while it was yet daylight, started at a pre-arranged rate of forty miles per hour. Seymour was reached in due average time, but before the soldiers had time to step upon the platform, came the not altogether unexpected, though disappointing, news that the gun was no longer required, as the whole of the outlaws had been taken. The train proceeded no further, and the gun, officers, and men returned by the first passenger goods-train to Melbourne.

On Saturday night, at six o'clock, the Chief Secretary was informed by telegram of the murder at Sebastopol, and he at once communicated with Captain Standish, Chief Commissioner of Police, with whom he consulted. Seeing the gravity of the situation, and remembering how previously the gang had always managed to obtain a good start of the police after the commission of their outrages, it was decided to despatch a special train to Beechworth at once. The Minister of Railways was informed of that determination, and without delay a train was got in readiness. Superintendent Hare, who was at Benalla, was telegraphed to, and instructed to proceed to Beechworth, and the black trackers, under Lieutenant O'Connor, who were at Essendon, where they were staying previously to their return to Queensland, were also apprised of the fact that they were required. As their engagement to the Victorian Government had expired, Captain Standish telegraphed to the Commissioner of Police at Brisbane, and requested that they might be allowed to remain, but that permission was refused. Mr. Ramsay, however, would not allow the Government to be so curtly treated, and he communicated with Mr. Palmer, Chief Secretary of Queensland, and at two o'clock on Sunday morning he obtained the required permit.

In the meantime—at about a quarter to ten—the train left Spencer Street with the tracking party. At a later period of the day—about nine a.m.—when the news of the commencement of the fight at Glenrowan was received, the Commissioner and the Chief Secretary again consulted, and it was then arranged that a reinforcement of police should be despatched, and an ample supply of ammunition was ordered to be sent up with it. As it would be almost impossible for any firing to take place without some of the men being injured, it was considered necessary that an experienced surgeon should also be sent to the scene, and accordingly Dr. Charles Ryan, who, it is well known, was attached to the medical staff at Plevna during the Russo-Turkish war and the bombardment of that town, was requested to place his services at the disposal of the authorities. He consented, and at about ten o'clock another special, taking Captain Standish, Dr. Ryan, Senior-constable Walsh and five other constables, and a quantity of ammunition, left for Glenrowan. The circumstances of the wounding of Superintendent Hare, and the commencement of the attack; that Ned Kelly had been wounded and captured; that he had been discovered to be wearing a breastplate of iron, a mask, and helmet; that his wounds were not considered to be mortal, were all duly telegraphed.

At twenty minutes to eleven a.m., it was officially intimated that the civilians had been liberated from the hotel; that Byrne had been shot; and that Dan Kelly and Hart maintained possession, and were firing in reply to the incessant firing by the police. As there appeared to be every likelihood that, if the fight was continued, some of the police might be seriously injured, the Chief

Secretary instructed Captain Standish, if possible, to blow the house up, but before doing so to see that none but members of the gang were in it. Colonel Anderson was summoned to a consultation with a view to steps being taken to effect that object, and the result was that at twenty minutes past two p.m. a third special, conveying that officer and a detachment of artillery, with a 12-pounder field-piece, left for Glenrowan, but as the termination of the conflict before the arrival of the train at Benalla rendered it unnecessary that it should proceed further, it was detained at that place. The Chief Secretary also advised by telegram that a wooden bullet-proof shield should be constructed to be fitted on a dray or wagon, under cover of which the attacking party might approach the house and effect its ruin, always assuming that the gang were the sole occupants. It was also feared by Mr. Ramsay that the fight would not be concluded before nightfall, and that if that was so, the outlaws might escape in the dark. He therefore consulted with Mr. Ellery, the Government astronomer, and asked his advice as to the practicability of sending up an electric-light apparatus, but that gentleman expressed the opinion that it would be of little utility adopting such a

GROUP TAKEN DURING THE FIGHT.

CONGRATULATIONS. 309

course, as it would take quite twenty-four hours after the apparatus arrived on the ground to get it fairly at work. To carry out the same idea, however, Mr. Ramsay telegraphed suggesting that large bonfires should be burnt round the house so as to give the required light and prevent the bushrangers escaping. But all these precautions were not required to be put in practice, as before sundown the final scene in the tragedy had been enacted.

His Excellency the Governor telegraphed about noon to Superintendent Hare, congratulating him on the bravery displayed by himself and his men, and encouraging them in the struggle in which they were engaged. The Chief Secretary, on behalf of the Government, also telegraphed to Mr. Hare to the same effect; and at twenty minutes past one p.m., Sir Henry Parkes, Premier of the Government of New South Wales, telegraphed to the Victorian Government, expressing the great satisfaction which was experienced in Sydney at the prospect of a speedy destruction of the gang, and congratulating the Government.

The change which had been lately made in the control of the police in the Kelly district gave rise at the time it was decided upon to some comment.

Mr. Ramsay states that on assuming office he made the determination that, if possible, the Kellys should be discovered without delay. He accordingly summoned Assistant-Commissioner Nicholson, who was in charge of the police in the district, and told him of the dissatisfaction which was experienced at the absence of results from the presence of the force there. He reminded him that he had been there for ten months, but that nothing had been done, and said that unless within a reasonable time something definite was effected or ascertained, an alteration of the arrangements would be made. Mr. Nicholson requested to be allowed a month longer, but he eventually returned to his position as Assistant-Commissioner at Melbourne.

Mr. Hare, who had been engaged in the capture of Power, the notorious bushranger, was spoken to as to his filling the vacancy. In Mr. Ramsay's opinion he had been very badly treated, inasmuch as he had not received any recognition of the services he had rendered to the colony on that occasion. He had had his salary increased by £100 a year at the time that Superintendent Winch's was also added to, but under the *régime* of the late Government his salary had been reduced by Parliament, whilst Mr. Winch's was continued. He was regarded as being specially qualified for the duty which he was required to perform, and he was instructed to choose the best men and officers in the force with whom to act. He was further assured that he would be untrammelled by any official rules and regulations.

The Chief Secretary received a later telegram from the Chief Secretary of Queensland in the forenoon, which stated that from what had been reported officially, and had been communicated by residents of Queensland who had visited Victoria, it appeared that a considerable amount of jealousy was evinced by the Victorian police with respect to the trackers, and that unless they were allowed to go to the front at once, it was little use their being required to do so, because if the white police preceded them and effaced the tracks, they could not do their work.

The outlaws were disposed of in time to give the police a claim to the reward of £8000 offered by the Governments of Victoria and New South Wales. For it was notified on the 20th of April that the reward would be withdrawn on the 20th of July.

At the inquest on the body of Aaron Sherritt, held at the Vine Hotel, Beechworth, before Mr. W. H. Foster, P.M., the jury having been empanelled, the following evidence was heard:—

John Sherritt, father of deceased, deposed that he had seen the body of the deceased, and identified it as that of his son Aaron, aged twenty-five years. He did not know from his personal knowledge how his son came by his death.

William Sherritt, brother of the deceased, identified the body as that of his brother, but did not know from personal knowledge how he came by his death.

Ellen Barry stated—" I am deceased's mother-in-law, and identify the body as that of my late son-in-law. I was at Aaron Sherritt's house on Saturday last, and was present at his death. I was at the house between six and seven o'clock, half an hour before the outlaws arrived. There were also my daughter and the deceased present. I was sitting at the fire when we heard a knock at the door. The deceased and his wife were having tea. There was a candle alight in the room in which I was sitting. An ordinary knock was given at the back-door, that being the first sign we got of any one being about. Aaron answered the knock, and said, 'Who's there?' and he heard Antone Wicks reply, 'I have lost my road, Sherritt; come and put me on the road.' I heard no other noise at the time. The deceased then opened the door and put his head out. I heard something said outside, but could not say what. The deceased appeared to be inclined to step back into the room, but before he could retreat a shot was fired from outside—by whom I do not know. The shot was fired very close to the door, and as soon as deceased was struck he stepped backwards into the centre of the room. After the first shot, Joe Byrne stepped up to the door and fired a second shot at the deceased, who was still standing in the centre of the room. Deceased then fell back to the ground. Byrne remained at the door for a short time. My daughter then asked, 'Joe, why did you shoot Aaron?' and Byrne replied, 'If I did not, he would shoot me.' Byrne, who had a gun in his hand, was in sight during the whole of the conversation. Byrne then told me to open the door opposite the one at which he stood. I did so, and saw Dan Kelly outside with a gun in his hand. I was then allowed to go outside. When outside Byrne asked me, 'Is there a window in front of the house?' I said, 'Yes,' and Byrne called out, 'Look out, Dan; there is a window in the front of the house.' Dan Kelly then joined me and Byrne, and I recognized him. He afterwards returned to the front of the house. About five or ten minutes elapsed from the time I heard the knock until I saw Dan Kelly. Two shots had been fired by Byrne before I went outside, and he afterwards fired two shots at the bedroom. Byrne was directly in front of the house when he fired at the bedroom."

CHAPTER XIV.

The Outlaws' Plans—Execution of Ned Kelly—Habits and Customs of the Gang—Katie Kelly's behaviour—Kelly's distrust of Hart—The Cost of the Destruction of the Gang.

IT was noticed by the constables who surrounded the hotel that a number of horses, saddled and bridled, were ready to be used by the outlaws; some of them were horses recently reported as stolen, and others were those which we had frequently seen ridden by Kelly's sisters. The constables shot some of them so as to prevent the escape of the outlaws. The prisoners were allowed out soon after daylight, and when the last of them came away, only Steve Hart and Dan Kelly were alive in the hotel. The police say Hart and Dan Kelly kept firing out of the windows up to one or two o'clock in the day, but having the armour on they were unable to take accurate aim. I have no hesitation in saying that had they been without armour when we first attacked them at the hotel, and could have taken proper aim at us, not one of us could have escaped being shot.

They were obliged to hold the rifle at arm's-length to get anything of a sight. When I was hit I had my arm under my gun and was running towards them; they were on my right front, the butt of my gun was under my elbow with the left hand under the barrels, ready to be used in a moment. Had it been an inch higher or lower it would have missed me.

The outlaws had provided themselves with another set of horses on the opposite side of the railway, so that had they been obliged to cross the line in a hurry, they would have been able to mount their horses and get off in a moment. The plan they arranged was as follows:—

Joe Byrne and Dan Kelly went to Woolshed to shoot Aaron Sherritt on Saturday night, whilst Ned and Steve Hart were to go to Glenrowan and pull up the rails. They knew it was our habit, whenever they showed themselves in any part of the distict, inmediately to get a special train and go to the spot and start on their tracks. They knew, therefore, directly the news reached Benalla that Sherritt was shot, I should start off with a party of police and black trackers to pick up their trail. No trains ran on that line on Sundays; therefore, the only one likely to come along would be a "special," with a party of police. There was no telegraph station at Glenrowan, and the special would not stop there. They thought that the train would get up great speed going down the incline after passing Glenrowan, and it would be smashed up and most of the party killed. They were then to jump on to their horses and go to the spot, and finish off those who had escaped.

The line was taken up about half a mile from Glenrowan. They would then have started off to Benalla, robbed all the banks, and probably secured £4000 or £5000. If they had worn their armour with overcoats they might have been shot at fifty times without being injured. They had arranged to have placed one of their number on the bridge in Benalla, so as to prevent any person giving information concerning them. The police were all on the opposite side of the river, and it was their intention to blow up the railway bridge at Benalla, so as to stop the traffic on the line. I believe they had a keg of gunpowder and fuse ready for the purpose at Glenrowan.

This was what Mrs. Byrne alluded to when she said they were about "to do something that would astonish not only all the colonies, but the whole world." Had they succeeded in wrecking our train that morning, there would have been fearful carnage afterwards. There is no question of doubt that at

Glenrowan they had parties of scouts, both in the hotel and outside of it; most of them, no doubt, were their own relations, and their name was legion. The Kellys were very short of cash when they stuck up Glenrowan. Their sisters were in debt everywhere, and they were compelled to make a raid in order to get money.

About a fortnight before they were captured, I was speaking to the owner of a hotel not far from Glenrowan. He told me the outlaws were in debt to him to the amount of £26. I asked him how he ever expected to be paid. He replied—" Oh, they will get another bank some of these days." I said to him, "I suppose you will be very sorry when they are captured?" "No," he said, "I won't. I am getting tired of them. They give us a lot of trouble—destroy our fences and injure our property, and we dare not say a word about it. If we did we would only get the worst of it."

Notwithstanding all Kelly's boasted pluck and bounce, how game he would die, &c., he was the only one who in any way showed the white feather. When the constables ran up to him after Steele had hold of him, he begged for mercy, and asked them to spare his life. There is no doubt that, had he been able to walk, he would have gone off, leaving

EXECUTION OF NED KELLY.

his comrades behind him in the hotel. It was always said that Dan Kelly was the most bloodthirsty wretch of the whole gang, and that Ned had the greatest difficulty in restraining him from shooting every person he came across.

After the building was burnt, the charred remains of Dan Kelly and Steve Hart were pulled out of the fire and were given over to their relatives; Joe Byrne's remains were taken to Benalla, and an inquest held on them. Ned Kelly was taken to Benalla, and next day he was forwarded to the Melbourne gaol, where he was for some weeks under the care of Dr. Shields. Subsequently he was sent up to Beechworth, where he was committed for trial, and then sent back to Melbourne, where he was tried and sentenced to be hanged. He had quite recovered from his wounds before he was executed. He was allowed to see his mother, who was an inmate in the Melbourne gaol, the day before his execution, and say good-bye to her. Her last words to him were, "Mind you die like a Kelly." The coroner who held the inquest on Ned Kelly told me he seldom saw a man show so little pluck, and if it had not been for his priest, who kept him up, he would not have been able to walk to the gallows.

As for myself, I was sent to Melbourne the day after the fight, under the care of Dr. Ryan, who bestowed the greatest attention on me for some months. My wound was more serious than I thought. To use the words of the Police Commission—" In the very first volley Superintendent Hare received a bullet wound in the left wrist which rendered his arm useless. The ball passed through the limb, shattering the bone and severing the artery."

I should like to add a few remarks as to the origin of this outbreak and the disordered state of the district. For years this part of the colony had been infested with horse and cattle-stealers. The number of relations which the Kelly family possessed all over the colony was surprising. There was hardly a district in Victoria, and also in some parts of New South Wales, that they could not have found a blood-relation to have assisted in harbouring them. Joe Byrne was better educated than any of his companions. He was very fond of writing, and was a bit of a poet. A great deal of his writings fell into our hands. They were chiefly directed against the police. Aaron Sherritt told me that when they contemplated committing a robbery, such as sticking up a bank, Byrne wrote down the contemplated plan, and then the party decided what part each of them was to take in the affair. They were most particular about where they camped not to leave any marks behind them.

On one occasion, when talking to Aaron, I inadvertently broke a twig off a tree and began breaking up the leaves. He immediately stopped me, and said, "You would never do for a bushranger." I said, "Why not?" He replied, "If Ned Kelly saw any of his men break a twig off a tree when he was camped, he would have an awful row with them." When the outlaws travelled on horseback they never carried anything beyond one overcoat. This had to cover them day and night, and it seemed to me wonderful that men could exist in this manner. Sherritt quite astonished me by the way in which he used to dress in the coldest weather. I asked him if the Kellys were as hardy as he was, and could do without sleep as he could. He said that Ned Kelly was ten times as hardy.

Under the altered conditions which now exist, and the progress of settlement, there is no likelihood of another Kelly episode in the history of the colony.

I hardly think any one out of Australia could possibly conceive the hardships that men of this stamp can endure. They have an extraordinary way of sleeping; they coil themselves up like dogs. I remember one night finding Aaron on my doormat, about one o'clock in the morning. He came to my quarters, and not finding me, he lay down and fell asleep; his head appeared between his knees, and he said, when camping out he always slept in that position. He could go without sleep for a longer period than any other man I ever met, and he said that the Kellys could do the same. It was doubtless a most fortunate occurrence that Aaron was shot by the outlaws; it was impossible to reclaim him, and the Government of the colony would not have assisted him in any way, and he would have gone back to his old course of life, and probably spent his days in gaol, or he might have turned bushranger himself, when he would have been quite as dangerous a man as Edward Kelly. The Government gave his widow a comfortable allowance, and she was much better off without him. Katie Kelly, no doubt, was a most loyal sister to her brothers, and must have sacrificed a great deal for them; day and night she was always on the alert, and assisting them in every possible way. Of course she was very flash, and liked being noticed. When appearing in any of the townships, she always rode a good horse and wore a lot of jewellery; but it was noticed that if there was a long interval between the bank robberies, the jewellery disappeared. Katie behaved in a most disgusting manner after Ned was hanged; the evening of his execution in Melbourne she appeared on the stage of a music-hall with a bunch of flowers in her hand, together with her brother Jim, and exhibited herself to the public on payment of a shilling entrance-fee. When the curtain rose, she smiled and bowed to the audience, and felt proud of having so much notice taken of her. The Government put a stop to these exhibitions, and she afterwards went to Sydney, but she was not allowed to exhibit herself there either. The notes stolen from Euroa by the outlaws were very soon afterwards circulated amongst their friends. They were aware the numbers of the notes were not known, and persons passing them could not be convicted of receiving stolen property; and all debts incurred by their relations were at once paid with National Bank notes, which were, without doubt, the proceeds of the robbery. Subsequently the bank authorities took the numbers of all notes sent to their country branches, so as to endeavour, if possible, should another robbery take place, to be able to trace them. But in this case there was a further point in which the officials failed, for they neglected to take the numbers of the notes they paid over the counter, and when the stolen notes got into circulation, they found they bore the same numbers as those sent from Sydney to Jerilderie, but they could not swear they had not been paid over the counter.

It was currently reported that Steve Hart, who was a very undersized man, was in the habit of riding about the country dressed as a woman. I never believed it, and I feel sure Ned Kelly would not have trusted him away from himself, for fear of his surrendering and turning informer against his companions. Wherever Ned Kelly was seen, Hart was always with him, and Byrne and Dan Kelly went together. The horses stolen from the police at Jerilderie were some months afterwards found in the mountains at the head of the King river in Victoria, which the gang were known to frequent. It was a strange coincidence that none of the rifles stolen by the outlaws from the police at Jerilderie or the Wombat ranges were used by them at Glenrowan, but they had most inferior and obsolete repeating-rifles which had been cut short, and no proper aim could be taken with them, as they were not sighted.

Jerilderie is about 120 miles from Benalla and

the outlaws, with a change of horses, could have been back in their hiding-places in thirty-six hours after they left Jerilderie. Possibly they would ride by night only, and lie in the thick scrub during the day. Parties of police were sent out to watch the different crossing-places directly we received information of the robbery; but at that season of the year, the Murray being low, there were dozens of places where they could cross, and no one knew the river better than they did, and in consequence they were able to return without being interfered with.

I need hardly say that the cost of the search for, and the subsequent destruction of, the Kelly gang came to a very large sum. Mounted constables were brought from all parts of Victoria and stationed in the Kelly country; besides, special men were engaged, and many incidental expenses incurred. After the destruction of the gang a return was asked for in the Legislative Assembly showing the cost of effecting the capture of the outlaws, and it was then stated that a sum of thirty or forty thousand pounds had been spent; whereas if the salaries and wages of those engaged in the search had been included in this estimate, the cost would have been over £115,000—a large price to pay for the capture of four desperadoes and the destruction of a gang of malefactors. However, this apparently excessive expenditure on a series of thief-catching expeditions has had results which reach further, and are of much greater value to the colony of Victoria; for the habitual criminal in Australia has been taught that, however romantic and exciting the career of the bushranger may appear, as a trade bushranging "does not pay"; while the criminal classes have been shown that the Government of the colony is not to be played with, that crime will be followed up and put down with a determined hand, and that no considerations of economy, no saving of trouble, no sacrifice of time, energy, or even life will be allowed to stand in the way when the law has to be upheld by the Executive. To the wisdom of such a policy let this fact bear witness—The execution of the last of the Kelly gang destroyed the "Last of the Bushrangers."

THE END.

Lightning Source UK Ltd.
Milton Keynes UK
UKHW022145190522
403168UK00016B/536